GREAT GRAPH ART
to Build Early Math Skills

by Cindi Mitchell

D1482192

SCHOLASTIC
PROFESSIONAL BOOKS

NEW YORK • TORONTO • LONDON • AUCKLAND • SYDNEY
MEXICO CITY • NEW DELHI • HONG KONG • BUENOS AIRES

This book is dedicated to Arlene Garrison:
friend, soul mate, and, according to Navajo tradition,
newest member of our family.

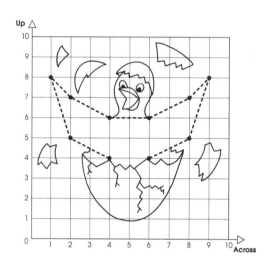

Cover design by Pamela Simmons and Norma Ortiz
Interior design by Solutions by Design, Inc.
Interior art by Kate Flanagan

ISBN: 0-439-14611-9

Copyright © 2001 by Cindi Mitchell.

Published by Scholastic Inc.
All rights reserved. Printed in the U.S.A.

Contents

Easy Coordinate Graphing With Addition and Subtraction

Introduction

Welcome to Great Graph Art to Build Early Math Skills!

Mathematics is the foundation for creating many forms of art, such as kaleidoscopes, quilts, tapestries, weavings, and graphic designs. This book was created to give children opportunities to use mathematics to create art in the form of graphs.

In the activities that follow, your students will enjoy plotting ordered pairs to create delightful pictures. In the process, they will learn a lot about graphing and, in many of the activities, practice addition and subtraction facts. They will also discover that math is more than basic computation—in fact, math is about creativity, art, and fun!

How to Use This Book

This book is divided into three sections:

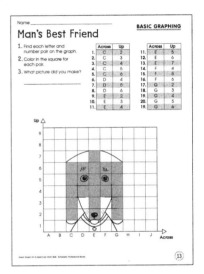

⚙ The first section, Basic Graphing, is the most simple and is designed for students who are beginning to learn graphing. They color squares based on ordered pairs, each of which contains a letter and a number. For example, in Man's Best Friend on page 13, students first find the square on the graph that corresponds with the ordered pair (C, 2) and then lightly color in that square. Students continue with the remaining ordered pairs. Voilà—a dog!

⚙ In the second section, students practice standard coordinate graphing. They find points on the graph based on a set of ordered pairs. Then, using a straightedge, they connect the points in the order they plotted them to make a picture. For example, in Let It Snow! on page 31, students first plot the point on the graph that corresponds with the ordered pair (7, 1). They then plot the point for the second ordered pair (7, 3) and use a straightedge to connect the two points. They continue in this manner to create a happy snowman.

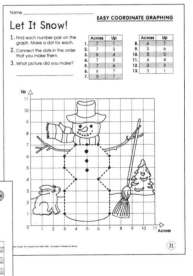

⚙ In the last section, students first solve simple addition or subtraction problems to determine the ordered pairs. (The skill focus of each activity appears at the top of each page.) Then they plot the pairs, in order, on the graph and use a straightedge to connect the points in the order they plotted them.

How to Begin

Choose one or two activity pages in the first section (pages 7–23) to introduce and teach basic coordinate graphing. After students thoroughly understand the process, let them do the coordinate graphing activities in Section Two. Finally, give them the opportunity to practice addition and subtraction facts in Section Three and find coordinate points based on the answers.

Taking It Further

After children have finished graphing the pictures, let them add their personal, creative touch by coloring them with crayons, markers, or colored pencils. Invite students to add drawings in the foreground and background or enhance the pictures by adding details. Then display the picture graphs in a prominent place in your classroom.

To extend children's graph art experience, invite students who are up for a challenge to come up with their own sets of math problems and accompanying graph pictures for classmates to solve and create. (Use the blank template on page 60.)

- To make a graph art picture like those in Section One, students draw a simple picture that fills complete squares on the graph. Inside each square, have them write in parentheses the ordered pair that identifies it. Then have students prepare a worksheet. On a separate sheet of paper, students can write the ordered pairs.

- To make a graph art picture like those in Sections Two and Three, students make a picture that has no more than nine or ten points. Beside each point, have them write in parentheses the ordered pair that identifies it. Then have students prepare a worksheet. On a separate sheet of paper, students can write the ordered pairs in the order they should be connected. Students may also choose to come up with addition and subtraction problems that, when solved, provide the two numbers in each ordered pair.

- Now the fun begins. Give each student a blank copy of the graph on page 60. Let students swap their completed worksheet pages with a classmate and try to re-create each other's original designs!

Cindi Mitchell

Name _____

First Number

1. Find each letter and number pair on the graph.

2. Color in the square for each pair.

3. What picture did you make?

_____

	Across	Up
1.	D	2
2.	D	8
3.	E	2
4.	E	3
5.	E	4
6.	E	5
7.	E	6
8.	E	7
9.	E	8
10.	F	2

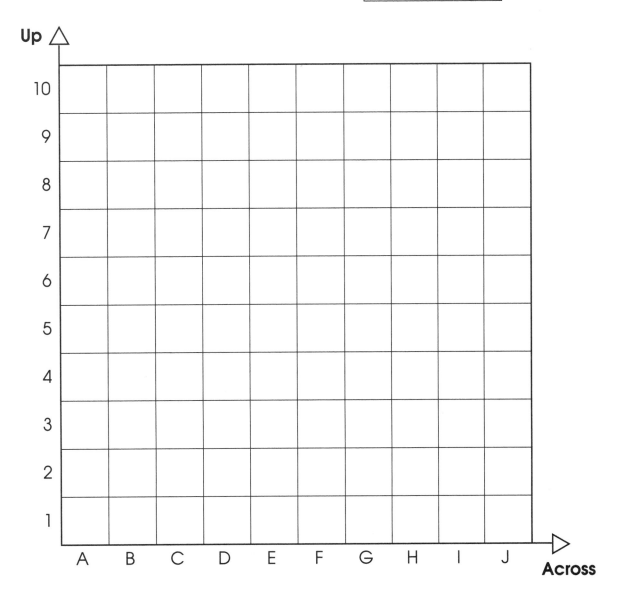

School Supplies

1. Find each letter and number pair on the graph.

2. Color a yellow square for each pair.

3. What picture did you make?

_____

	Across	Up
1.	C	4
2.	C	5
3.	D	4
4.	D	5
5.	E	4
6.	E	5
7.	F	4

	Across	Up
8.	F	5
9.	G	4
10.	G	5
11.	H	4
12.	H	5
13.	I	4
14.	I	5

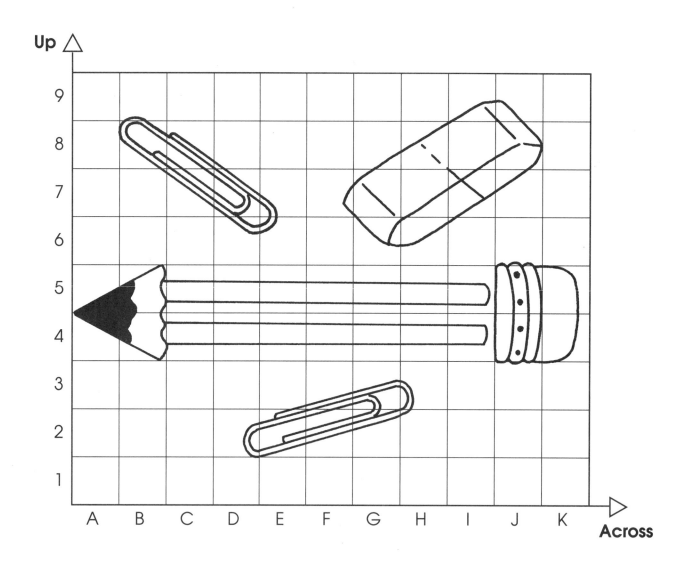

Up ▲

9 8 7 6 5 4 3 2 1

A B C D E F G H I J K   Across ▷

Name _____

Giant Shovel

1. Find each letter and number pair on the graph.

2. Color in the square for each pair.

3. What picture did you make?

_____

	Across	Up			Across	Up
1.	B	4		7.	C	7
2.	B	5		8.	D	4
3.	B	6		9.	D	7
4.	C	4		10.	E	4
5.	C	5		11.	G	5
6.	C	6		12.	H	5

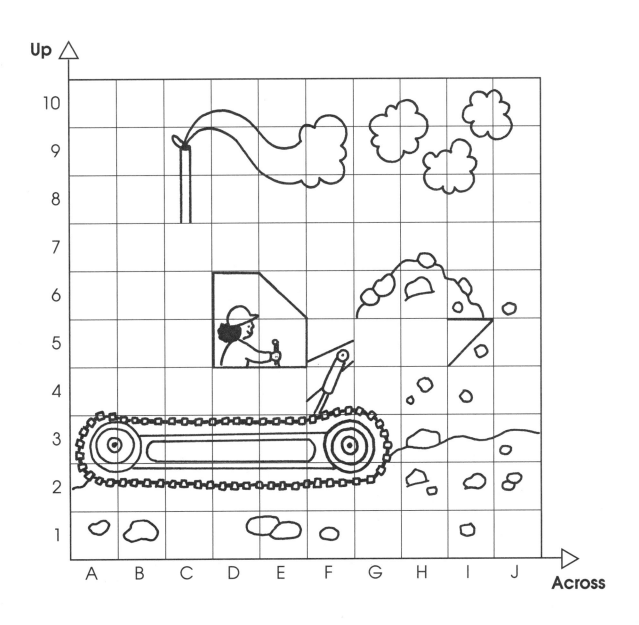

Name _____

Make a Wish!

1. Find each letter and number pair on the graph.

2. Color in the square for each pair.

3. What picture did you make?

_____

	Across	Up
1.	C	3
2.	C	4
3.	C	5
4.	C	6
5.	D	3
6.	D	4
7.	D	5
8.	D	6
9.	D	7
10.	E	3
11.	E	4
12.	E	5
13.	E	6
14.	E	7

	Across	Up
15.	F	3
16.	F	4
17.	F	5
18.	F	6
19.	F	7
20.	G	3
21.	G	4
22.	G	5
23.	G	6
24.	G	7
25.	H	3
26.	H	4
27.	H	5
28.	H	6

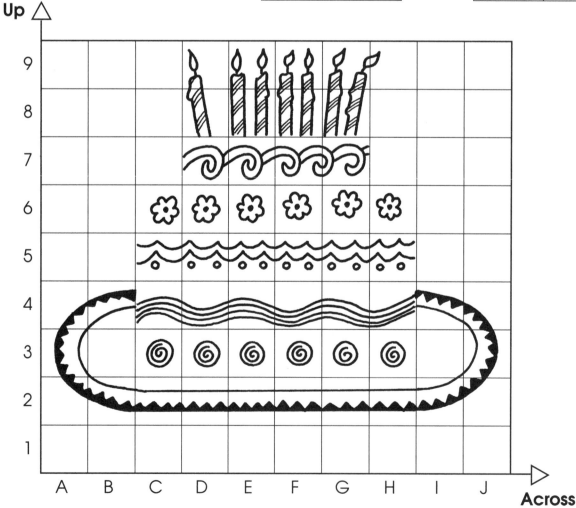

Great Graph Art to Build Early Math Skills Scholastic Professional Books

Name _____

Wiggle Worm

1. Find each letter and number pair on the graph.

2. Color in the square for each pair.

3. What picture did you make?

_____

	Across	Up
1.	B	2
2.	B	3
3.	B	4
4.	B	5
5.	C	2
6.	D	2
7.	D	3
8.	D	4
9.	D	5
10.	D	6
11.	E	6
12.	F	2
13.	F	3
14.	F	4

	Across	Up
15.	F	5
16.	F	6
17.	G	2
18.	H	2
19.	H	3
20.	H	4
21.	H	5
22.	H	6
23.	I	6
24.	J	2
25.	J	3
26.	J	4
27.	J	5
28.	J	6

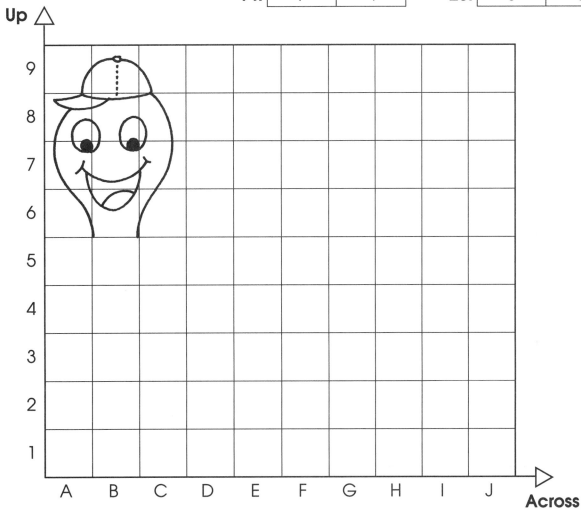

Name _____

Friendly Greeting

1. Find each letter and number pair on the graph.

2. Color in the square for each pair.

3. What picture did you make?

_____

	Across	Up
1.	B	3
2.	B	4
3.	B	5
4.	B	6
5.	B	7
6.	C	5
7.	D	3
8.	D	4
9.	D	5
10.	D	6
11.	D	7
12.	F	3

	Across	Up
13.	F	7
14.	G	3
15.	G	4
16.	G	5
17.	G	6
18.	G	7
19.	H	3
20.	H	7
21.	J	3
22.	J	5
23.	J	6
24.	J	7

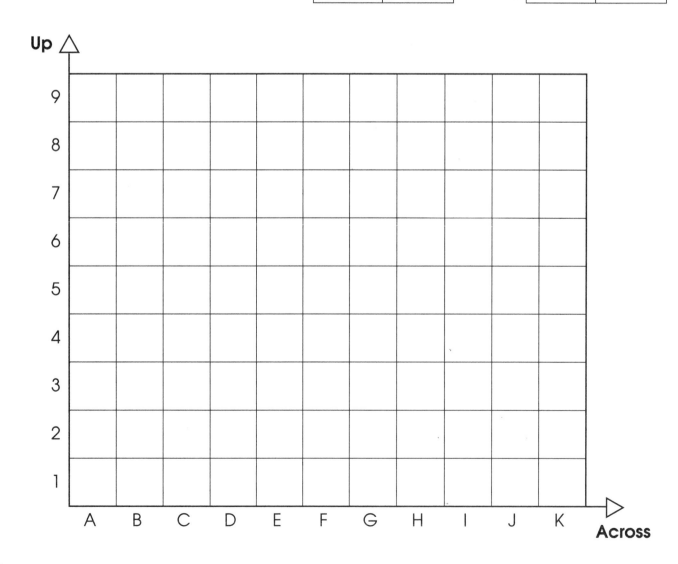

Up

9 8 7 6 5 4 3 2 1

A B C D E F G H I J K

Across

Name _____

Man's Best Friend

1. Find each letter and number pair on the graph.

2. Color in the square for each pair.

3. What picture did you make?

_____

	Across	Up
1.	C	2
2.	C	3
3.	C	4
4.	C	5
5.	C	6
6.	D	4
7.	D	5
8.	D	6
9.	E	2
10.	E	3
11.	E	4

	Across	Up
12.	E	5
13.	E	6
14.	E	7
15.	F	4
16.	F	5
17.	F	6
18.	G	2
19.	G	3
20.	G	4
21.	G	5
22.	G	6

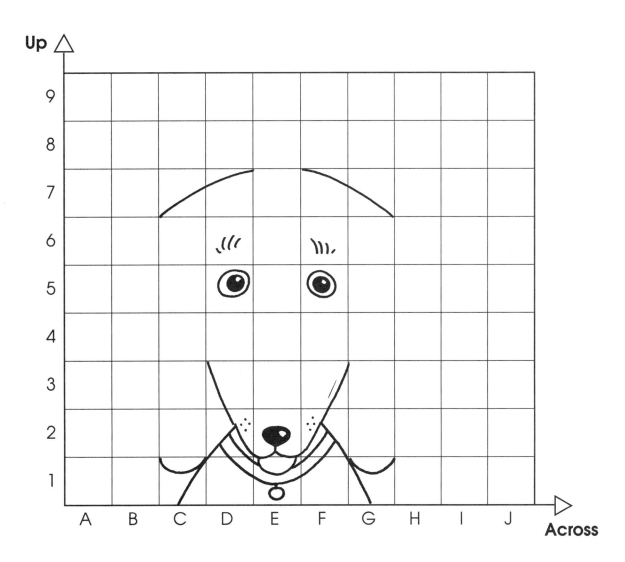

BASIC GRAPHING

Mystery Letter

1. Find each letter and number pair on the graph.

2. Color in the square for each pair.

3. What picture did you make?

_____

	Across	Up
1.	D	1
2.	D	2
3.	D	3
4.	D	4
5.	D	5
6.	D	6
7.	D	7
8.	D	8
9.	E	1
10.	E	4

	Across	Up
11.	E	5
12.	E	8
13.	F	1
14.	F	4
15.	F	5
16.	F	8
17.	G	2
18.	G	3
19.	G	6
20.	G	7

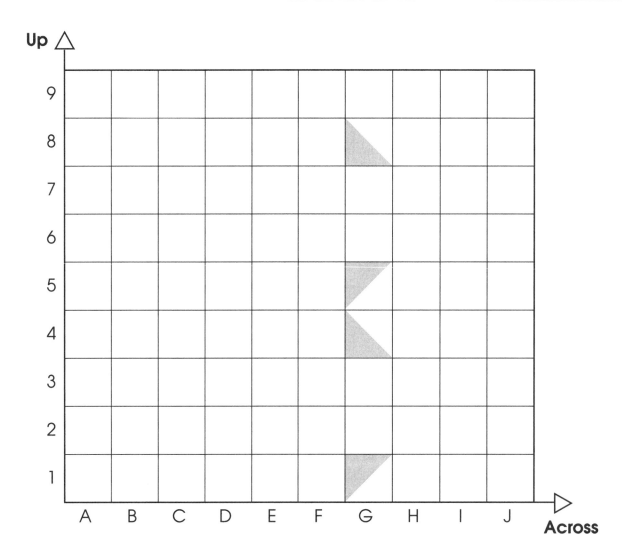

Great Graph Art to Build Early Math Skills Scholastic Professional Books

Name _____

Your Move

1. Find each letter and
number pair on the graph.

2. Color in the square for each pair.

3. What picture did you make?

_____

	Across	Up
1.	A	2
2.	A	4
3.	A	6
4.	A	8
5.	B	1
6.	B	3
7.	B	5
8.	B	7
9.	C	2
10.	C	4
11.	C	6
12.	C	8

	Across	Up
13.	D	1
14.	D	3
15.	D	5
16.	D	7
17.	E	2
18.	E	4
19.	E	6
20.	E	8
21.	F	1
22.	F	3
23.	F	5
24.	F	7

	Across	Up
25.	G	2
26.	G	4
27.	G	6
28.	G	8
29.	H	1
30.	H	3
31.	H	5
32.	H	7
33.	I	2
34.	I	4
35.	I	6
36.	I	8

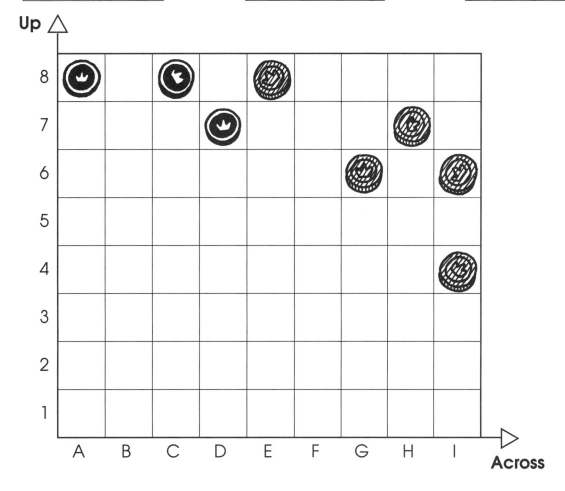

Name _____

Off to School!

1. Find each letter and number pair on the graph.

2. Color in the square for each pair.

3. What picture did you make?

_____

	Across	Up
1.	B	2
2.	B	3
3.	C	2
4.	C	3
5.	C	5
6.	D	2
7.	D	3
8.	D	4
9.	D	5
10.	E	2

	Across	Up
11.	E	3
12.	E	5
13.	F	2
14.	F	3
15.	F	4
16.	F	5
17.	G	2
18.	G	3
19.	G	5
20.	H	2

	Across	Up
21.	H	3
22.	H	4
23.	H	5
24.	I	2
25.	I	3
26.	I	5
27.	J	2
28.	J	3
29.	J	4
30.	J	5

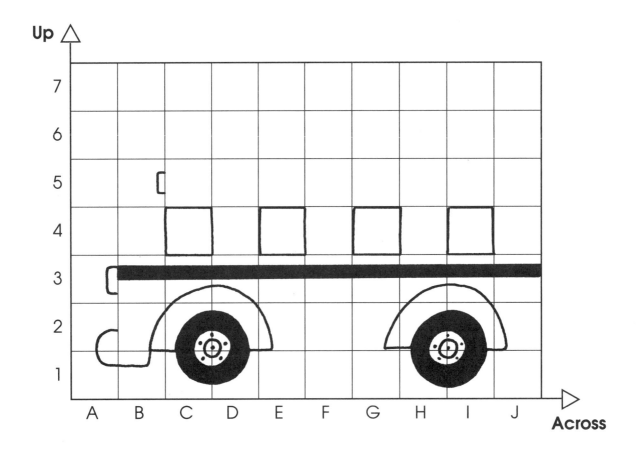

Great Graph Art to Build Early Math Skills   Scholastic Professional Books

Name _____

Skyline

1. Find each letter and number pair on the graph.

3. What picture did you make?

2. Color in the square for each pair.

_____

	Across	Up
1.	B	1
2.	B	2
3.	B	3
4.	B	4
5.	B	5
6.	C	1
7.	C	2
8.	C	3
9.	D	1
10.	D	2
11.	D	3
12.	D	4

	Across	Up
13.	D	5
14.	D	6
15.	E	1
16.	E	2
17.	E	3
18.	E	4
19.	E	5
20.	E	6
21.	F	1
22.	F	2
23.	G	1
24.	G	2

	Across	Up
25.	H	1
26.	H	2
27.	H	3
28.	H	4
29.	H	5
30.	H	6
31.	H	7
32.	I	1
33.	I	2
34.	I	3
35.	I	4

Name _____

Home Sweet Home

1. Find each letter and number pair on the graph.

2. Color in the square for each pair.

3. What picture did you make?

_____

	Across	Up
1.	C	1
2.	C	2
3.	C	3
4.	C	4
5.	D	3
6.	D	4
7.	D	5
8.	E	1
9.	E	2
10.	E	3
11.	E	4
12.	E	5

	Across	Up
13.	E	6
14.	F	1
15.	F	3
16.	F	4
17.	F	5
18.	G	1
19.	G	2
20.	G	3
21.	G	4
22.	G	5
23.	G	6

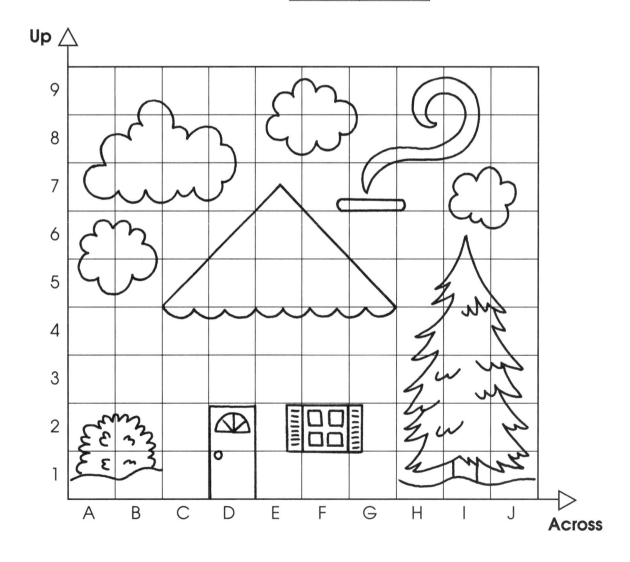

Great Graph Art to Build Early Math Skills Scholastic Professional Books

Name _____

Just for You

1. Find each letter and number pair on the graph.

2. Color in the square for each pair.

3. What picture did you make?

_____

	Across	Up
1.	D	2
2.	D	3
3.	D	4
4.	D	5
5.	D	6
6.	E	2
7.	E	3
8.	E	4
9.	E	5
10.	E	6
11.	E	7
12.	F	2
13.	F	3
14.	F	4

	Across	Up
15.	F	5
16.	F	6
17.	F	7
18.	G	2
19.	G	3
20.	G	4
21.	G	5
22.	G	6
23.	G	7
24.	H	3
25.	H	4
26.	H	5
27.	H	6
28.	H	7

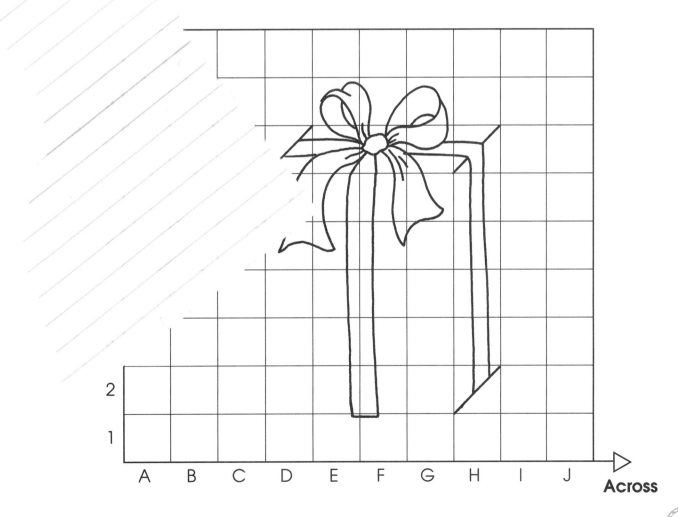

Across

Beautiful Swimmer

1. Find each letter and number pair on the graph.

2. Color in the square for each pair.

3. What picture did you make?

_____

	Across	Up
1.	C	3
2.	C	4
3.	C	5
4.	D	2
5.	D	3
6.	D	4
7.	D	5
8.	E	2
9.	E	3
10.	E	4
11.	F	2

	Across	Up
12.	F	3
13.	F	4
14.	G	2
15.	G	3
16.	G	4
17.	G	5
18.	G	6
19.	H	3
20.	H	6
21.	H	7

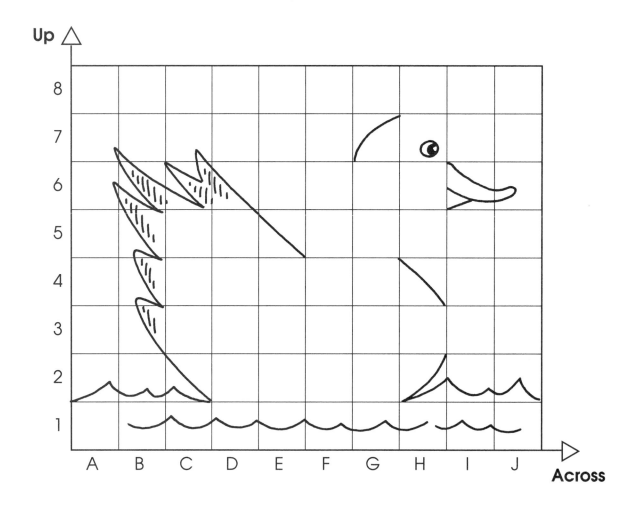

Great Graph Art to Build Early Math Skills Scholastic Professional Books

Name _____

Spinning Around

1. Find each letter and number pair on the graph.

2. Color in the square for each pair.

3. What picture did you make?

_____

	Across	Up
1.	D	1
2.	D	2
3.	D	3
4.	D	4
5.	D	5
6.	D	6
7.	D	7
8.	D	8
9.	E	1
10.	E	2
11.	E	3
12.	E	4
13.	E	5

	Across	Up
14.	E	6
15.	E	7
16.	E	8
17.	E	9
18.	F	1
19.	F	2
20.	F	3
21.	F	4
22.	F	5
23.	F	6
24.	F	7
25.	F	8

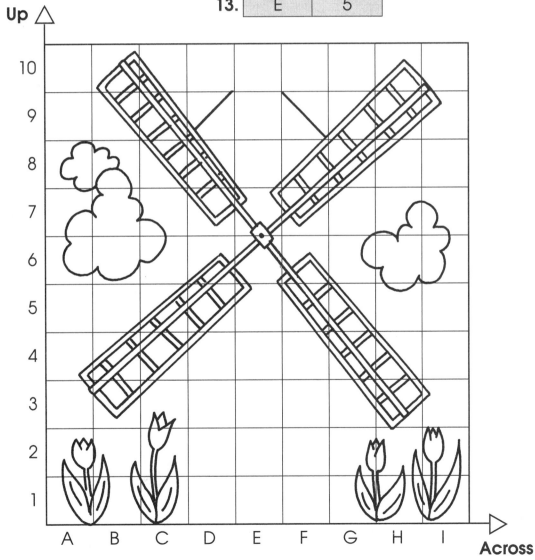

Name _____

There She Blows!

1. Find each letter and number pair on the graph.

2. Color in the square for each pair.

3. What picture did you make?

_____

	Across	Up
1.	B	3
2.	B	4
3.	B	5
4.	C	2
5.	C	3
6.	C	4
7.	C	5
8.	C	6
9.	D	2

	Across	Up
10.	D	3
11.	D	4
12.	D	5
13.	D	6
14.	E	2
15.	E	3
16.	E	4
17.	E	5
18.	E	6
19.	F	2
20.	F	3
21.	F	4

	Across	Up
22.	F	5
23.	F	6
24.	G	2
25.	G	3
26.	G	4
27.	G	5
28.	G	6
29.	H	3
30.	H	4
31.	H	5
32.	H	6
33.	H	7
34.	I	4
35.	I	5
36.	I	6
37.	I	7

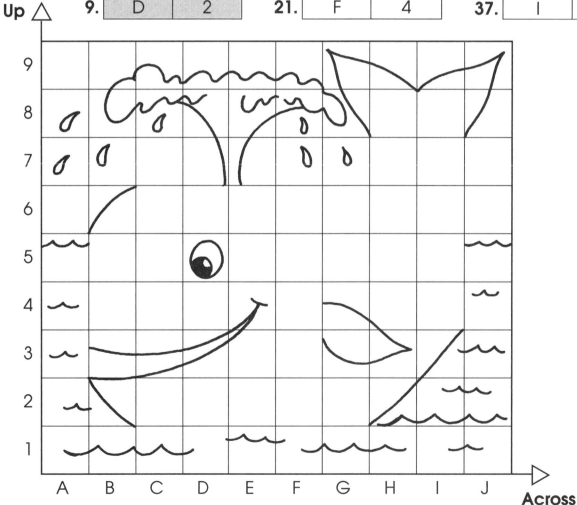

Great Graph Art to Build Early Math Skills Scholastic Professional Books

Name _____

Sail Away

1. Find each letter and number pair on the graph.

2. Color in the square for each pair.

3. What picture did you make?

_____

	Color these squares red.	
	Across	**Up**
1.	C	2
2.	D	1
3.	D	2
4.	E	1
5.	E	2
6.	F	1
7.	F	2
8.	G	2

	Color these squares blue.	
	Across	**Up**
9.	C	4
10.	C	5
11.	C	6
12.	C	7
13.	C	8
14.	C	9
15.	D	4
16.	D	5
17.	D	6
18.	D	7

	Color these squares blue.	
	Across	**Up**
19.	D	8
20.	E	4
21.	E	5
22.	E	6
23.	E	7
24.	F	4
25.	F	5
26.	F	6
27.	G	4
28.	G	5
29.	H	4

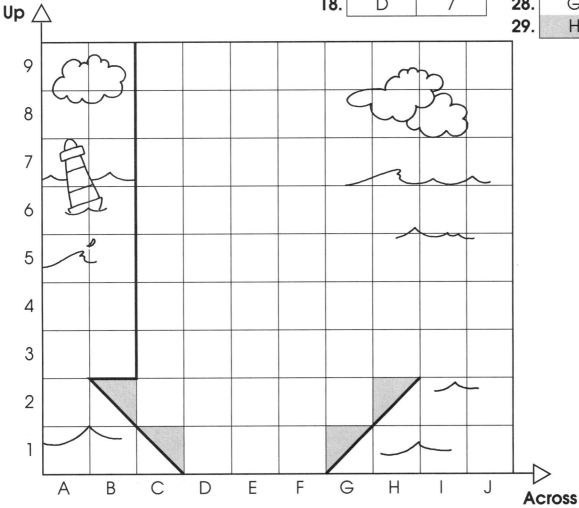

Spring Flower

1. Find each number pair on the graph. Make a dot for each.

2. Connect the dots in the order that you make them.

3. What picture did you make?

_____

	Across	Up
1.	6	7
2.	7	9
3.	7	6
4.	6	5
5.	5	5
6.	4	6
7.	4	9
8.	5	7

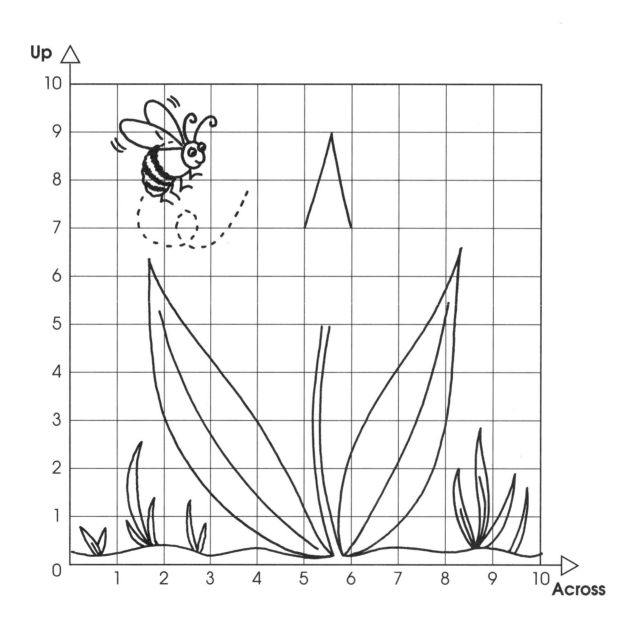

Great Graph Art to Build Early Math Skills Scholastic Professional Books

Name _____

Bright Light

1. Find each number pair on the graph. Make a dot for each.

2. Connect the dots in the order that you make them.

3. What picture did you make?

_____

	Across	Up
1.	5	4
2.	4	3
3.	4	1
4.	6	1
5.	6	3
6.	5	4
7.	5	5
8.	8	5
9.	6	9
10.	4	9
11.	2	5
12.	5	5

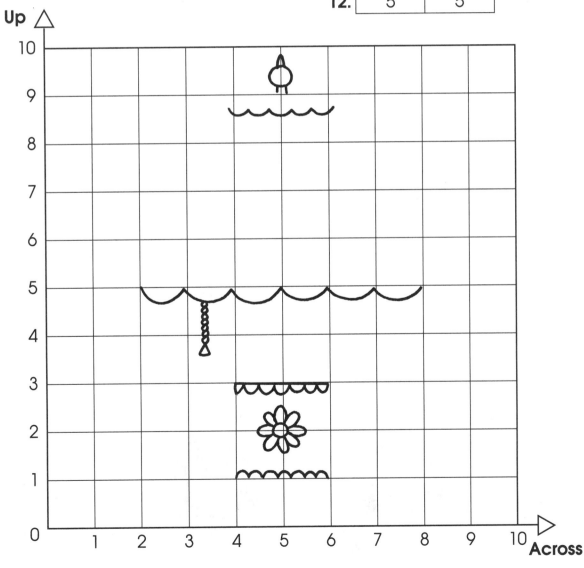

Name _____

Tow Truck

1. Find each number pair on the graph. Make a dot for each.

2. Connect the dots in the order that you make them.

3. What picture did you make?

_____

	Across	Up
1.	9	1
2.	9	5
3.	6	5
4.	10	8
5.	10	9
6.	6	6
7.	6	8
8.	5	9
9.	4	9
10.	3	8
11.	3	5
12.	1	4
13.	1	1

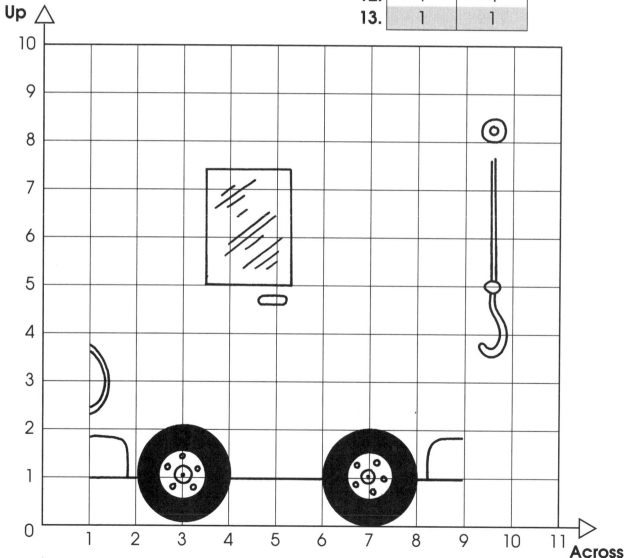

Great Graph Art to Build Early Math Skills Scholastic Professional Books

me _____

mmy Treat

nd each number pair on the
aph. Make a dot for each.

onnect the dots in the order
at you make them.

/hat picture did you make?

_____

	Across	Up
1.	3	2
2.	6	2
3.	8	4
4.	8	7
5.	6	9
6.	3	9
7.	1	7
8.	1	4
9.	3	2

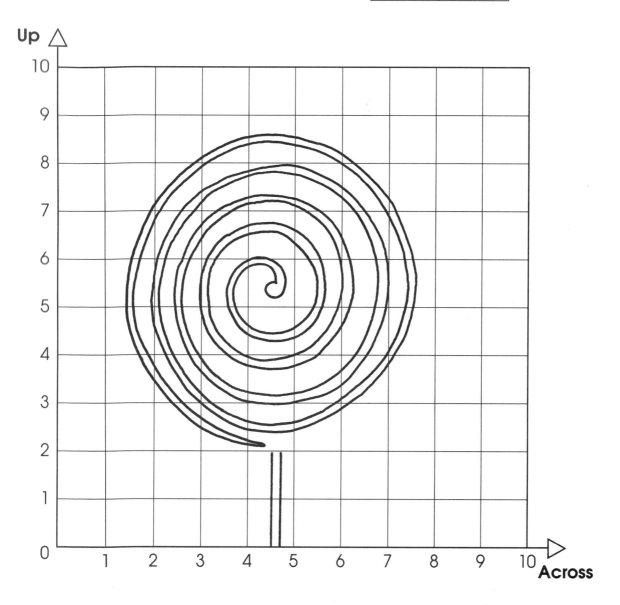

Name _____

Nam

Love

1. Find each number pair on the graph. Make a dot for each.

2. Connect the dots in the order that you make them.

3. What picture did you make?

_____

	Across	Up
1.	5	1
2.	7	3
3.	9	5
4.	9	7
5.	7	8
6.	5	7
7.	3	8
8.	1	7
9.	1	5
10.	3	3
11.	5	1

Yu

1. F
   g

2. C
   t

3. V

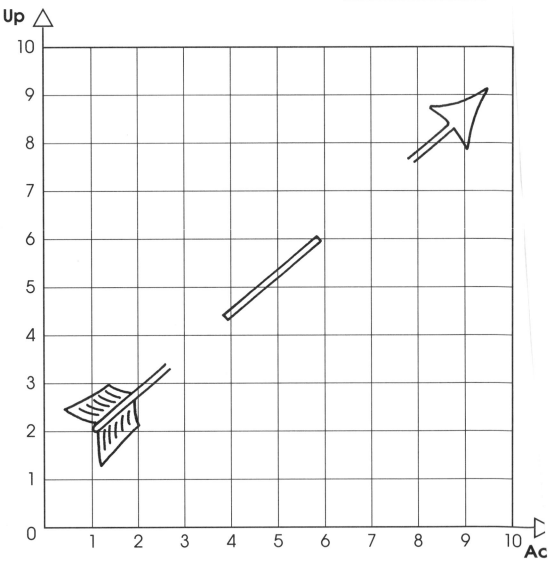

Name _____

Just Hatched

1. Find each number pair on the graph. Make a dot for each.

2. Connect the dots in the order that you make them.

3. What picture did you make?

_____

	Across	Up
1.	6	4
2.	8	5
3.	9	8
4.	8	7
5.	6	6
6.	4	6
7.	2	7
8.	1	8
9.	2	5
10.	4	4

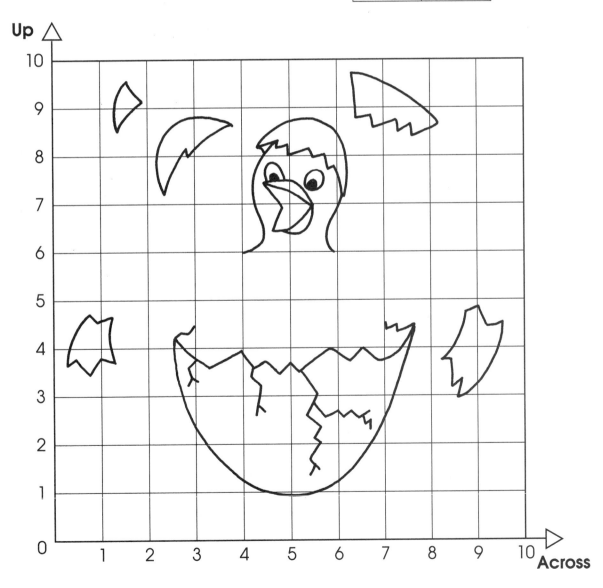

Name _____

Surprises!

1. Find each number pair on the graph. Make a dot for each.

2. Connect the dots in the order that you make them.

3. What picture did you make?

_____

	Across	Up
1.	9	2
2.	7	4
3.	8	4
4.	6	6
5.	7	6
6.	5	8
7.	3	6
8.	4	6
9.	2	4
10.	3	4
11.	1	2

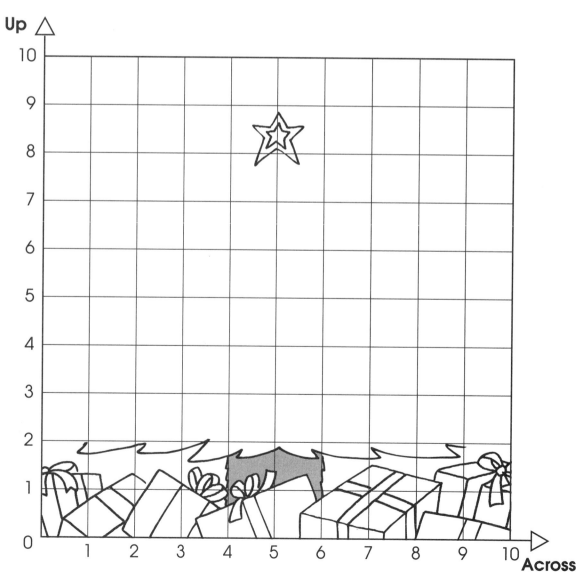

Great Graph Art to Build Early Math Skills Scholastic Professional Books

Name _____

Let It Snow!

1. Find each number pair on the graph. Make a dot for each.

2. Connect the dots in the order that you make them.

3. What picture did you make?

_____

	Across	Up
1.	7	1
2.	7	3
3.	6	4
4.	7	5
5.	7	6
6.	6	7
7.	5	7

	Across	Up
8.	4	7
9.	3	6
10.	3	5
11.	4	4
12.	3	3
13.	3	1

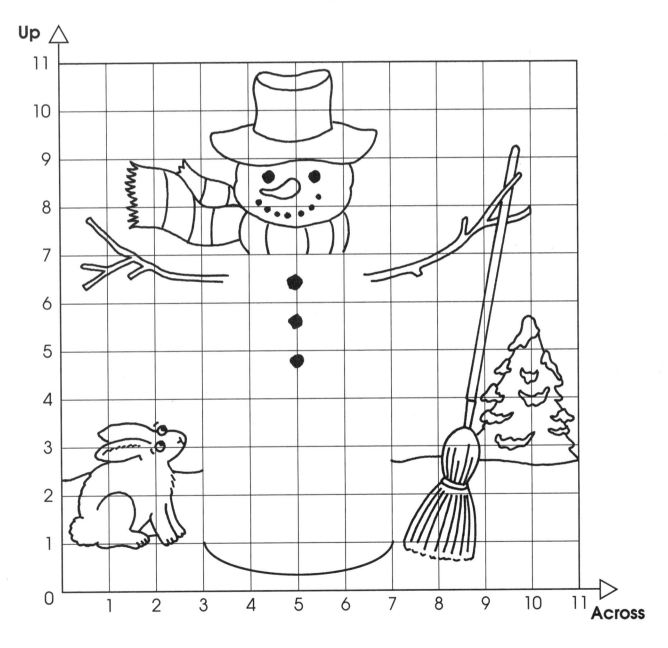

Name _____

Sparkling Diamond

1. Find each number pair on the graph. Make a dot for each.

2. Connect the dots in the order that you make them.

3. What picture did you make?

_____

	Across	Up
1.	5	0
2.	7	1
3.	8	3
4.	7	5
5.	5	6
6.	3	5
7.	2	3
8.	3	1
9.	5	0

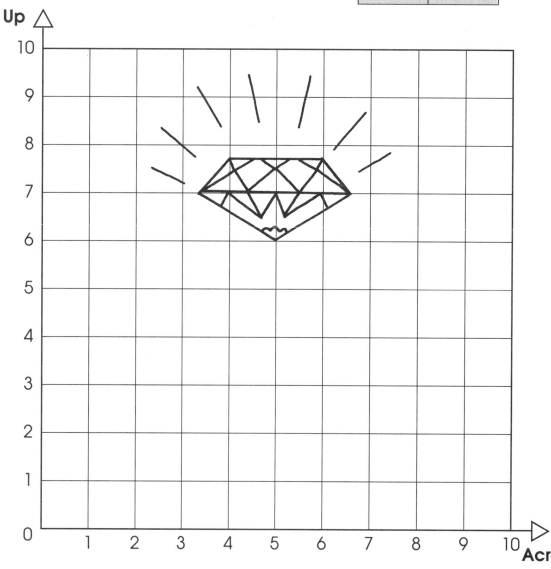

Great Graph Art to Build Early Math Skills Scholastic Professional Books

Name _____

Out for a Swim

1. Find each number pair on the graph. Make a dot for each.

2. Connect the dots in the order that you make them.

3. What picture did you make?

_____

	Across	Up
1.	10	4
2.	7	3
3.	6	3
4.	4	4
5.	2	5
6.	0	4
7.	1	6

	Across	Up
8.	0	8
9.	2	7
10.	5	6
11.	7	6
12.	8	6
13.	10	5

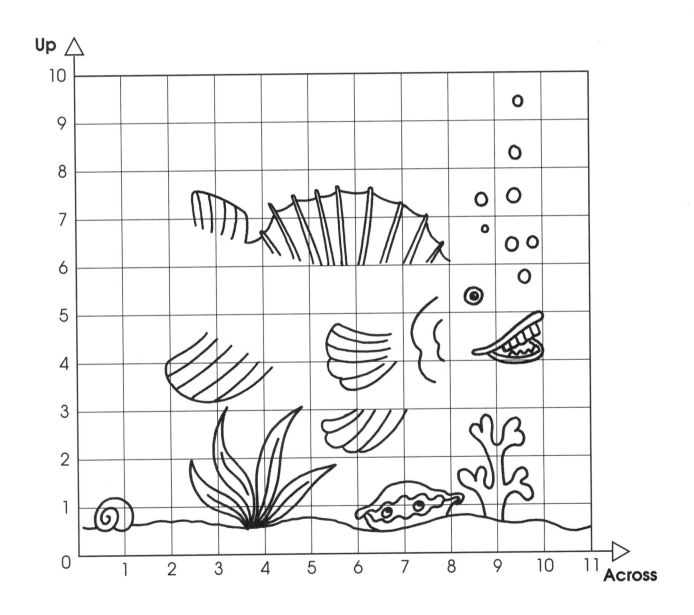

Bright Smile

1. Find each number pair on the graph. Make a dot for each.

2. Connect the dots in the order that you make them.

3. What picture did you make?

_____

	Across	Up
1.	9	3
2.	9	8
3.	10	8
4.	10	3
5.	9	3
6.	4	4
7.	3	5
8.	3	6
9.	4	7
10.	9	8

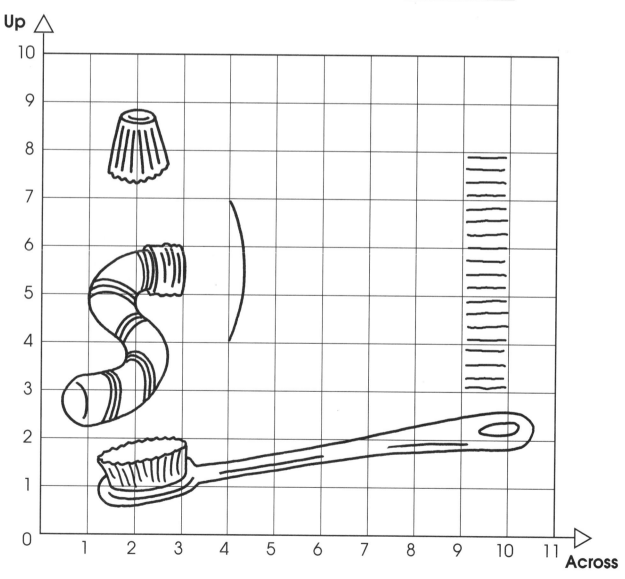

Name _____

Stars and Stripes

1. Find each number pair on the graph. Make a dot for each.

2. Connect the dots in the order that you make them.

3. What picture did you make?

_____

	Across	Up
1.	3	2
2.	4	2
3.	5	1
4.	6	1
5.	7	2
6.	8	2
7.	10	1
8.	10	7
9.	8	8
10.	7	7
11.	6	7
12.	5	8

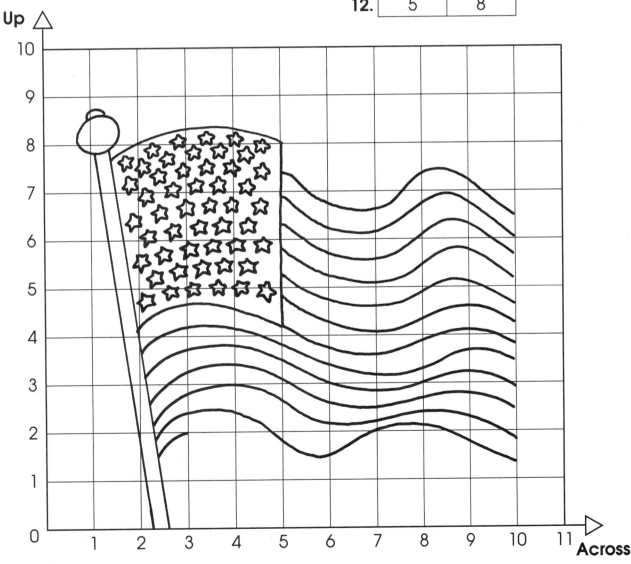

Name _____

Sprinkles on Top!

EASY COORDINATE GRAPHING

1. Find each number pair on the graph. Make a dot for each.

2. Connect the dots in the order that you make them.

3. What picture did you make?

_____

	Across	Up
1.	5	0
2.	6	3
3.	7	5
4.	8	6
5.	7	8
6.	5	9
7.	3	8
8.	2	6
9.	3	5
10.	4	3
11.	5	0

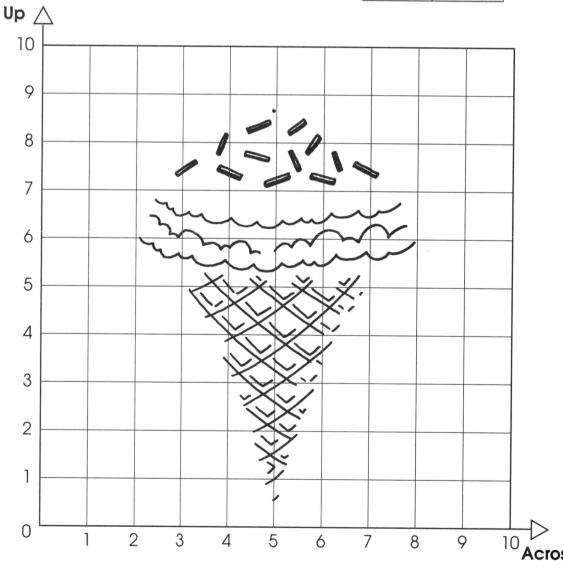

36

Name _____

Chug, Chug

1. Find each number pair on the graph. Make a dot for each.

2. Connect the dots in the order that you make them.

3. What picture did you make?

_____

	Across	Up
1.	0	1
2.	2	3
3.	2	6
4.	3	6
5.	3	7
6.	4	7
7.	4	6
8.	7	6
9.	7	9
10.	10	9
11.	10	1

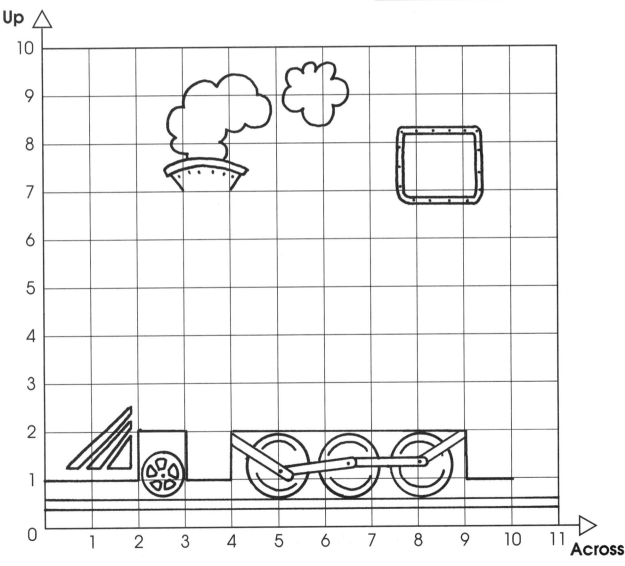

Name _____

Night-Light

EASY COORDINATE GRAPHING

1. Find each number pair on the graph. Make a dot for each.

2. Connect the dots in the order that you make them.

3. What picture did you make?

_____

	Across	Up
1.	6	11
2.	5	7
3.	1	7
4.	4	5
5.	3	0
6.	6	3
7.	9	0
8.	8	5
9.	11	7
10.	7	7
11.	6	11

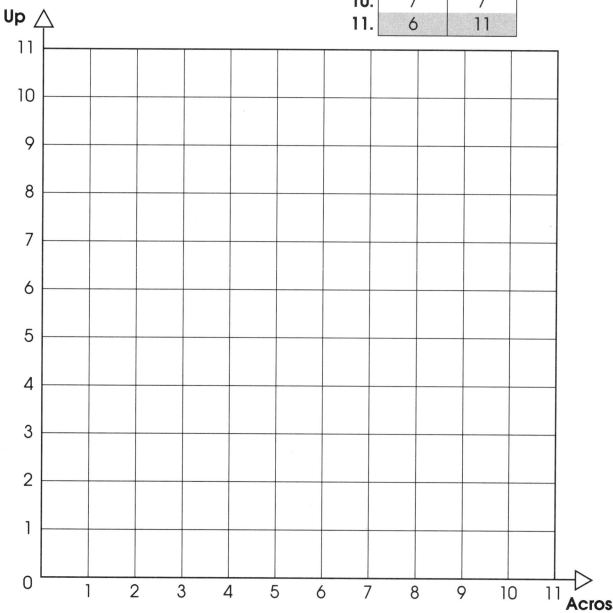

Name _____

Rain Showers

1. Find each number pair on the graph. Make a dot for each.

2. Connect the dots in the order that you make them.

3. What picture did you make?

_____

	Across	Up
1.	1	6
2.	2	5
3.	3	6
4.	4	5
5.	5	6
6.	6	5
7.	7	6
8.	8	5
9.	9	6
10.	5	10
11.	1	6

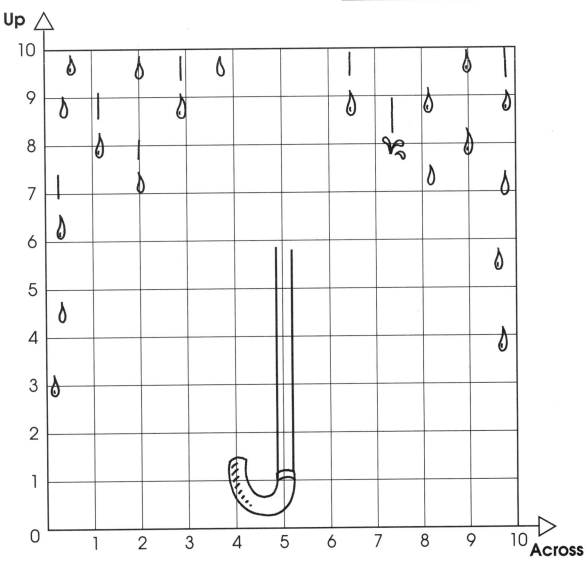

Name _____

Funny Face

1. Find each number pair on the graph. Make a dot for each.

2. Connect the dots in the order that you make them.

3. What picture did you make?

_____

	Across	Up
1.	5	2
2.	9	2
3.	8	4
4.	7	6
5.	6	8
6.	5	10

	Across	Up
7.	4	8
8.	3	6
9.	2	4
10.	1	2
11.	5	2

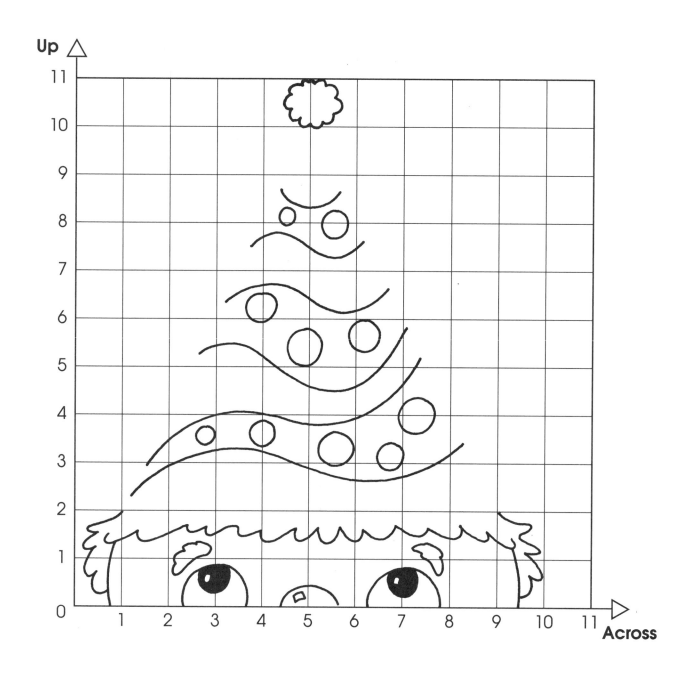

Great Graph Art to Build Early Math Skills Scholastic Professional Books

Name _____

Teatime

1. Find each number pair on the graph. Make a dot for each.

2. Connect the dots in the order that you make them.

3. What picture did you make?

_____

	Across	Up
1.	6	5
2.	7	4
3.	8	5
4.	9	5
5.	7	1
6.	6	0
7.	2	0
8.	1	1
9.	1	4
10.	2	5

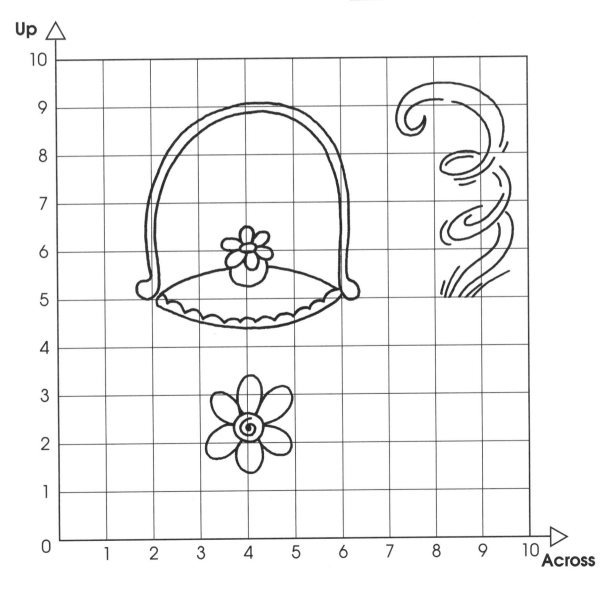

Curvy Letter

1. Find each number pair on the graph. Make a dot for each.

2. Connect the dots in the order that you make them.

3. What picture did you make?

_____

	Across	Up			Across	Up
1.	3	2		8.	3	9
2.	7	2		9.	3	5
3.	7	6		10.	6	5
4.	4	6		11.	6	3
5.	4	8		12.	3	3
6.	7	8		13.	3	2
7.	7	9				

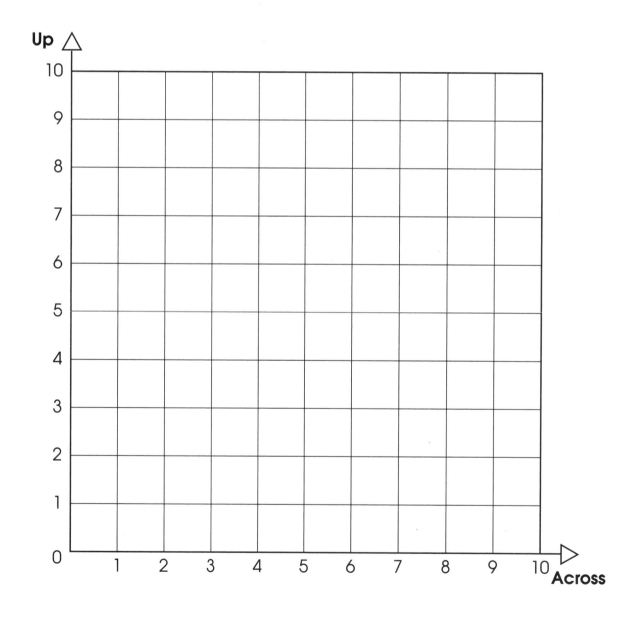

Great Graph Art to Build Early Math Skills Scholastic Professional Books

Name _____

Measure Up

1. Solve the problems.

2. Find each number pair on the graph. Make a dot for each.

3. Connect the dots in the order that you make them.

4. What picture did you make?

_____

	Across	Up
1.	1 + 0 = ____	1 + 2 = ____
2.	2 + 4 = ____	3 + 0 = ____
3.	5 + 5 = ____	2 + 1 = ____
4.	8 + 2 = ____	6 + 0 = ____
5.	3 + 3 = ____	5 + 1 = ____
6.	1 + 0 = ____	4 + 2 = ____
7.	0 + 1 = ____	0 + 3 = ____

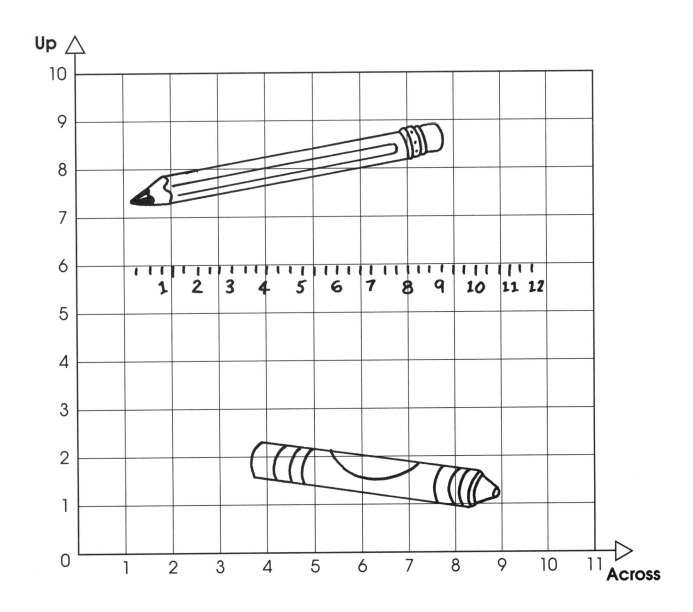

Highflier

1. Solve the problems.

2. Find each number pair on the graph. Make a dot for each.

3. Connect the dots in the order that you make them.

4. What picture did you make?

_____

	Across	Up
1.	3 + 3 = _____	2 + 0 = _____
2.	7 + 2 = _____	5 + 1 = _____
3.	4 + 4 = _____	5 + 5 = _____
4.	6 + 1 = _____	5 + 4 = _____
5.	1 + 5 = _____	0 + 8 = _____
6.	2 + 3 = _____	6 + 1 = _____
7.	2 + 4 = _____	1 + 1 = _____

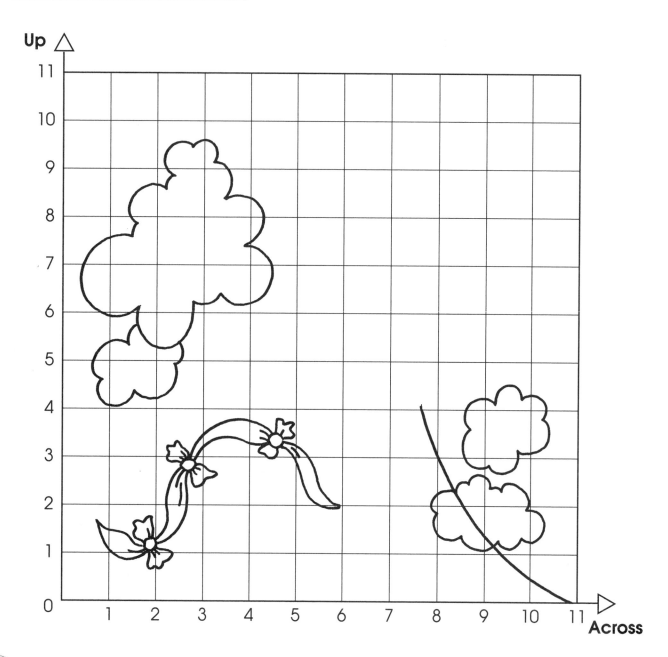

Great Graph Art to Build Early Math Skills Scholastic Professional Books

Juicy Fruit

1. Solve the problems.

2. Find each number pair on the graph. Make a dot for each.

3. Connect the dots in the order that you make them.

4. What picture did you make?

_____

	Across	Up
1.	9 + 9 = ____	8 + 6 = ____
2.	13 + 5 = ____	3 + 7 = ____
3.	2 +14 = ____	4 + 2 = ____
4.	4 + 8 = ____	1 + 3 = ____
5.	1 + 7 = ____	0 + 4 = ____
6.	2 + 2 = ____	5 + 1 = ____
7.	1 + 1 = ____	4 + 6 = ____

	Across	Up
8.	2 + 0 = ____	12 + 2 = ____
9.	3 + 1 = ____	8 + 2 = ____
10.	2 + 4 = ____	7 + 1 = ____
11.	5 + 3 = ____	3 + 3 = ____
12.	10 + 2 = ____	2 + 4 = ____
13.	13 + 1 = ____	4 + 4 = ____
14.	8 + 8 = ____	1 + 9 = ____
15.	6 +12 = ____	5 + 9 = ____

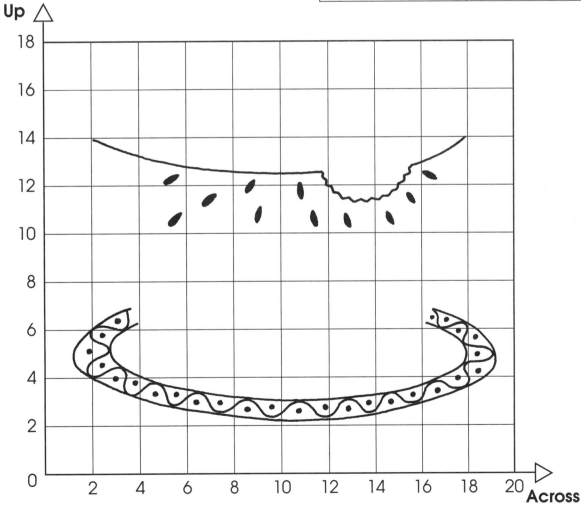

Name _____

Slowpoke Reptile

1. Solve the problems.

2. Find each number pair on the graph. Make a dot for each.

3. Connect the dots in the order that you make them.

4. What picture did you make?

_____

	Across	Up
1.	1 + 3 = _____	6 + 6 = _____
2.	4 + 2 = _____	8 + 8 = _____
3.	6 + 2 = _____	9 + 9 = _____
4.	9 + 3 = _____	10 + 8 = _____
5.	7 + 9 = _____	3 + 13 = _____
6.	12 + 6 = _____	3 + 5 = _____
7.	9 + 5 = _____	2 + 4 = _____
8.	7 + 1 = _____	5 + 1 = _____
9.	3 + 3 = _____	4 + 4 = _____

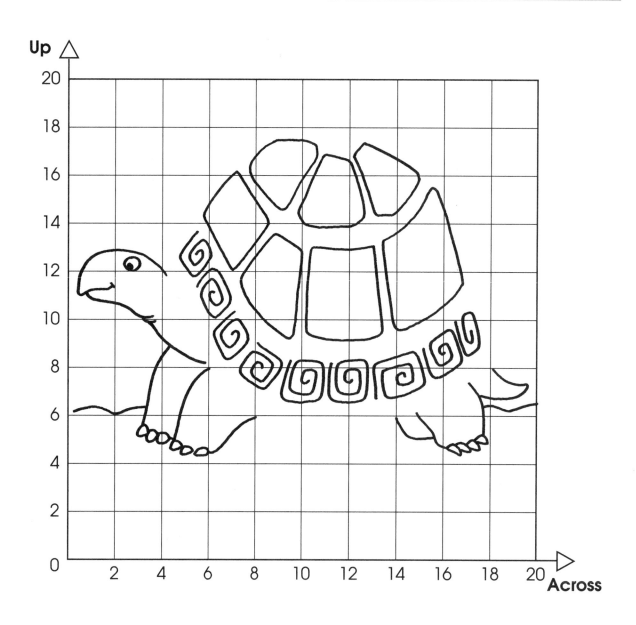

Great Graph Art to Build Early Math Skills Scholastic Professional Books

Name _____

Horsing Around

1. Solve the problems.

2. Find each number pair on the graph. Make a dot for each.

3. Connect the dots in the order that you make them.

4. What picture did you make?

_____

	Across	Up
1.	12 + 12 = _____	5 + 5 = _____
2.	19 + 3 = _____	3 + 9 = _____
3.	5 + 15 = _____	13 + 1 = _____
4.	2 + 16 = _____	10 + 6 = _____
5.	9 + 7 = _____	9 + 9 = _____
6.	7 + 7 = _____	18 + 2 = _____
7.	5 + 7 = _____	13 + 3 = _____

	Across	Up
8.	3 + 7 = _____	9 + 5 = _____
9.	1 + 1 = _____	1 + 3 = _____
10.	0 + 4 = _____	0 + 2 = _____
11.	2 + 6 = _____	1 + 1 = _____
12.	6 + 4 = _____	4 + 2 = _____
13.	8 + 8 = _____	3 + 5 = _____
14.	18 + 6 = _____	0 + 2 = _____

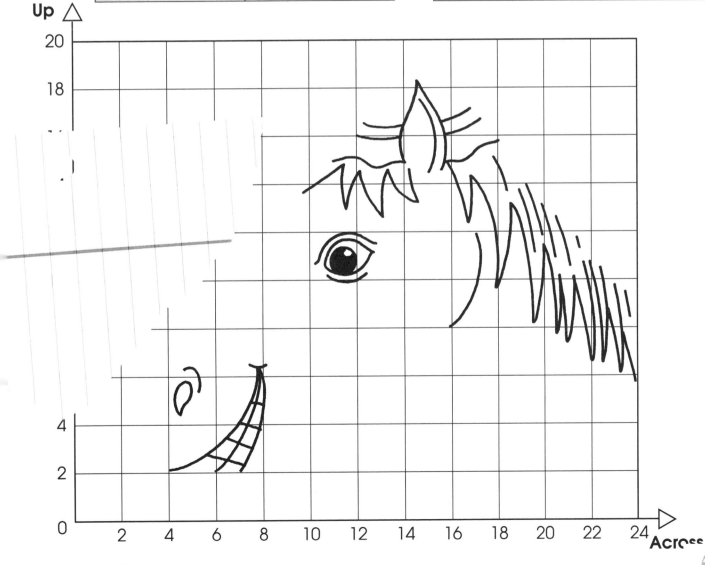

You've Got Mail!

1. Solve the problems.

2. Find each number pair on the graph. Make a dot for each.

3. Connect the dots in the order that you make them.

4. What picture did you make?

_____

	Across	Up
1.	20 + 7 = _____	12 + 12 = _____
2.	12 + 3 = _____	11 + 13 = _____
3.	1 + 2 = _____	10 + 14 = _____
4.	13 + 2 = _____	10 + 5 = _____
5.	13 + 14 = _____	21 + 3 = _____
6.	23 + 4 = _____	11 + 4 = _____
7.	5 + 22 = _____	2 + 4 = _____
8.	3 + 12 = _____	1 + 5 = _____
9.	3 + 0 = _____	6 + 0 = _____
10.	2 + 1 = _____	2 + 13 = _____
11.	0 + 3 = _____	2 + 22 = _____

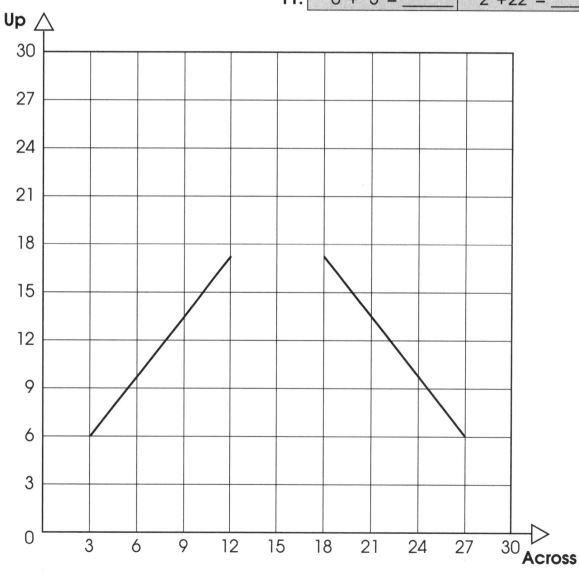

Great Graph Art to Build Early Math Skills Scholastic Professional Books

Name _____

Home From the Beach

1. Solve the problems.

2. Find each number pair on the graph. Make a dot for each.

3. Connect the dots in the order that you make them.

4. What picture did you make?

_____

	Across	Up
1.	13 + 2 = _____	2 + 4 = _____
2.	16 + 11 = _____	5 + 1 = _____
3.	12 + 15 = _____	14 + 4 = _____
4.	10 + 17 = _____	11 + 16 = _____
5.	3 + 12 = _____	14 + 13 = _____
6.	5 + 10 = _____	12 + 6 = _____
7.	11 + 4 = _____	4 + 2 = _____

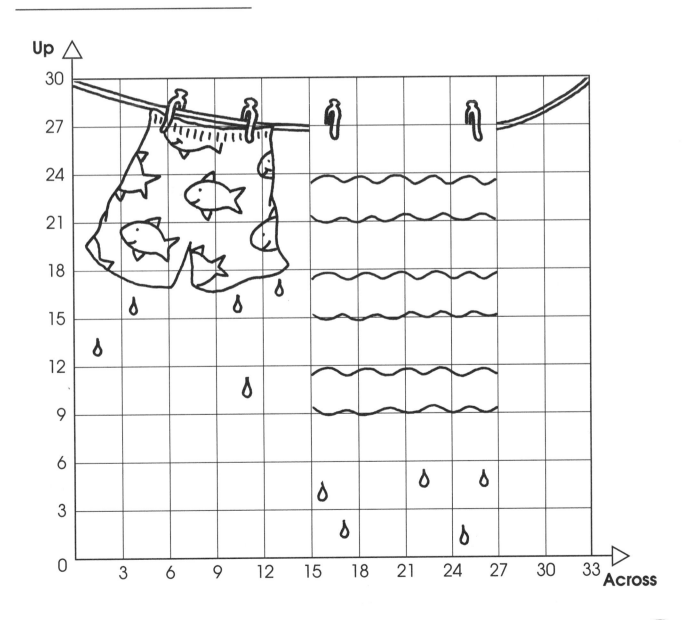

Name _____

Zoo Animal

1. Solve the problems.

2. Find each number pair on the graph. Make a dot for each.

3. Connect the dots in the order that you make them.

4. What picture did you make?

	Across	Up
1.	13 + 7 = _____	12 + 4 = _____
2.	15 + 9 = _____	5 + 3 = _____
3.	11 + 9 = _____	0 + 4 = _____
4.	19 + 9 = _____	2 + 2 = _____
5.	10 +18 = _____	11 + 5 = _____
6.	16 +16 = _____	9 + 7 = _____
7.	28 + 8 = _____	2 + 6 = _____

	Across	Up
8.	17 +15 = _____	1 + 3 = _____
9.	31 + 9 = _____	3 + 1 = _____
10.	8 +32 = _____	8 + 8 = _____
11.	19 +25 = _____	19 + 1 = _____
12.	27 +17 = _____	18 +14 = _____
13.	7 +29 = _____	17 +23 = _____
14.	18 + 6 = _____	25 +15 = _____

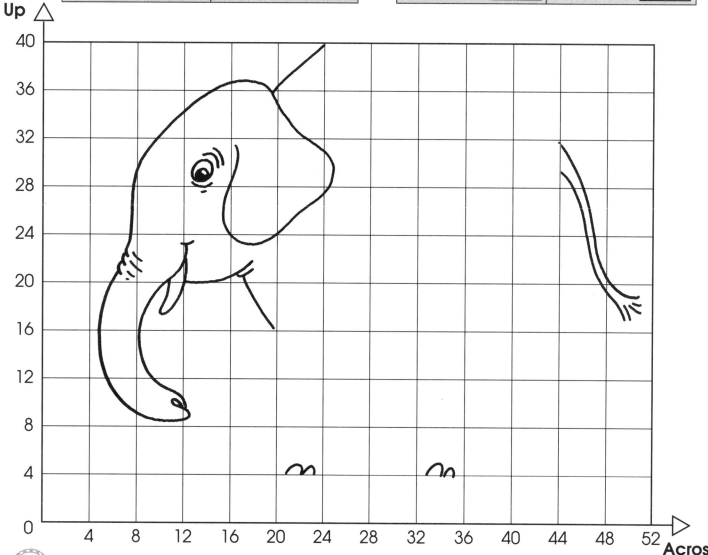

Name _____

Rich Man's Fish

1. Solve the problems.

2. Find each number pair on the graph. Make a dot for each.

3. Connect the dots in the order that you make them.

4. What picture did you make?

	Across	Up
1.	3 + 3 = _____	12 + 18 = _____
2.	10 + 2 = _____	9 + 9 = _____
3.	17 + 7 = _____	5 + 7 = _____
4.	17 + 19 = _____	4 + 8 = _____
5.	35 + 25 = _____	19 + 11 = _____
6.	53 + 19 = _____	6 + 6 = _____
7.	38 + 28 = _____	16 + 14 = _____

	Across	Up
8.	19 + 47 = _____	9 + 27 = _____
9.	26 + 46 = _____	16 + 38 = _____
10.	18 + 42 = _____	8 + 28 = _____
11.	18 + 18 = _____	17 + 37 = _____
12.	15 + 9 = _____	25 + 29 = _____
13.	3 + 9 = _____	29 + 19 = _____
14.	5 + 1 = _____	13 + 17 = _____

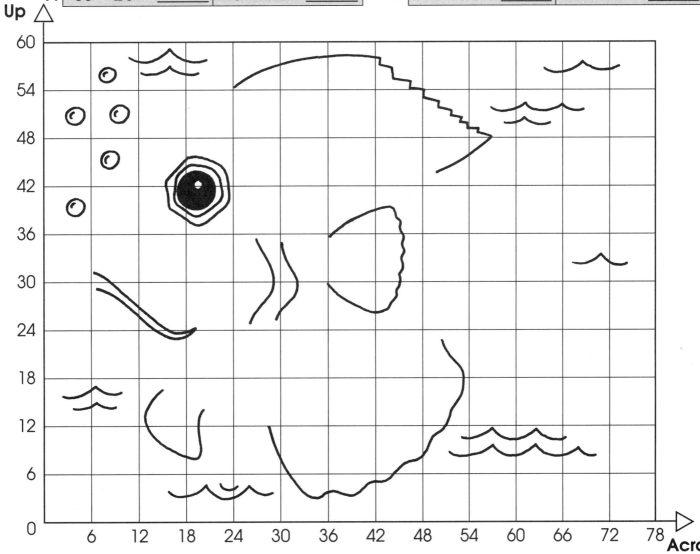

Up

60
54
48
42
36
30
24
18
12
6
0

6 12 18 24 30 36 42 48 54 60 66 72 78

Across

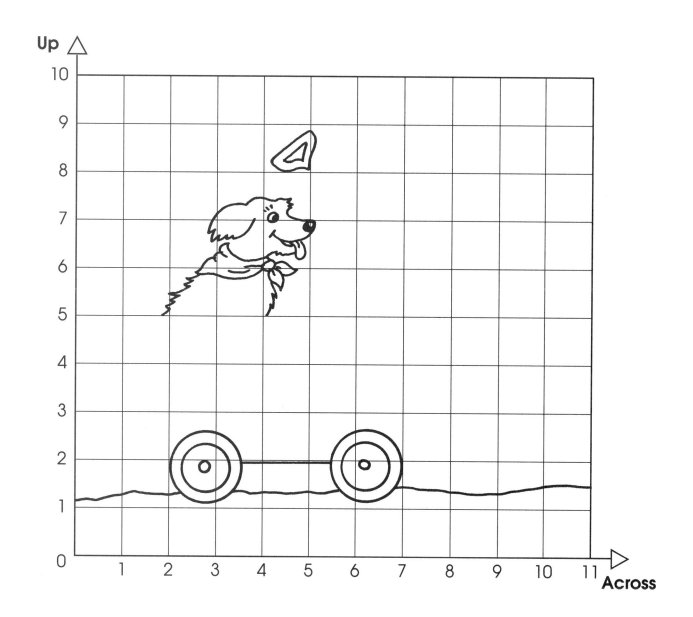

Name _____

Let's Go for a Ride

1. Solve the problems.

2. Find each number pair on the graph. Make a dot for each.

3. Connect the dots in the order that you make them.

4. What picture did you make?

_____

	Across	Up
1.	10 − 8 = ____	9 − 7 = ____
2.	6 − 5 = ____	3 − 1 = ____
3.	10 − 9 = ____	8 − 3 = ____
4.	9 − 2 = ____	7 − 2 = ____
5.	10 − 3 = ____	6 − 4 = ____
6.	9 − 1 = ____	8 − 6 = ____
7.	10 − 1 = ____	7 − 5 = ____
8.	6 − 1 = ____	10 − 2 = ____

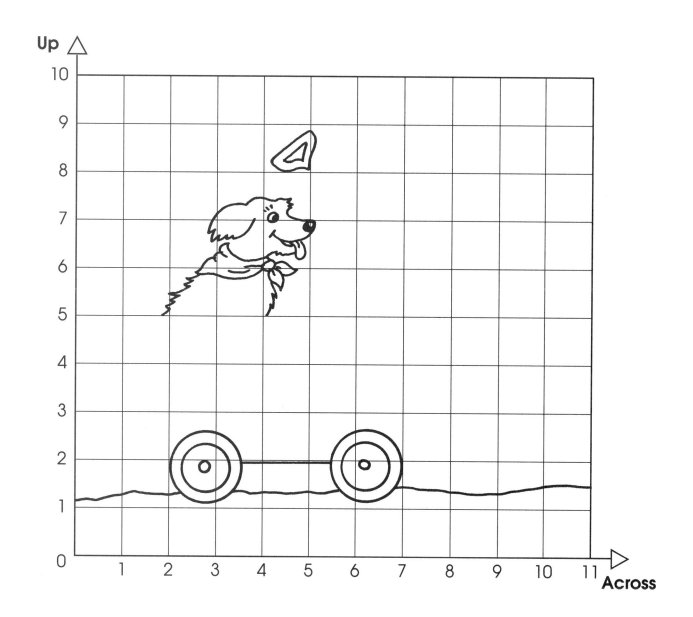

Great Graph Art to Build Early Math Skills   Scholastic Professional Books

Name _____

Chirp, Chirp!

1. Solve the problems.

2. Find each number pair on the graph. Make a dot for each.

3. Connect the dots in the order that you make them.

4. What picture did you make?

_____

	Across	Up
1.	10 − 7 = _____	10 − 8 = _____
2.	4 − 2 = _____	3 − 1 = _____
3.	7 − 5 = _____	1 − 0 = _____
4.	8 − 0 = _____	1 − 0 = _____
5.	9 − 1 = _____	8 − 6 = _____
6.	10 − 3 = _____	7 − 5 = _____
7.	10 − 2 = _____	8 − 2 = _____
8.	8 − 3 = _____	10 − 0 = _____
9.	9 − 7 = _____	7 − 1 = _____
10.	4 − 1 = _____	5 − 3 = _____
11.	9 − 2 = _____	6 − 4 = _____

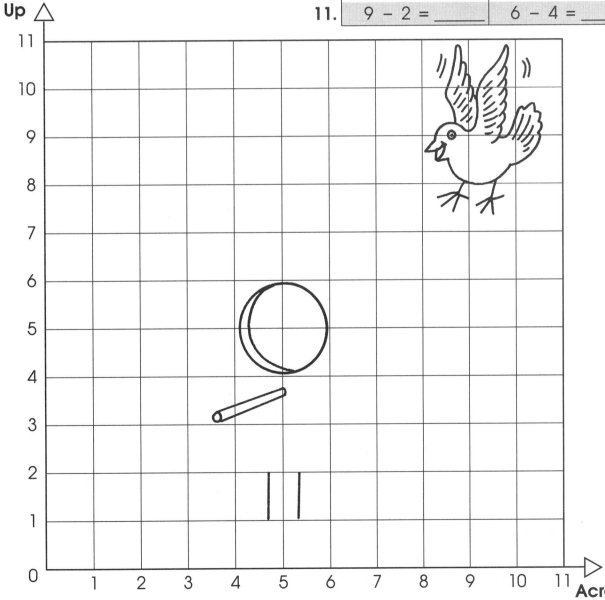

Name _____

Out of the Past

1. Solve the problems.
2. Find each number pair on the graph. Make a dot for each.

3. Connect the dots in the order that you make them.
4. What picture did you make?

_____

	Across	Up
1.	10 − 10 = _____	15 − 10 = _____
2.	6 − 5 = _____	14 − 8 = _____
3.	14 − 12 = _____	15 − 9 = _____
4.	11 − 7 = _____	13 − 5 = _____
5.	13 − 7 = _____	11 − 3 = _____
6.	15 − 8 = _____	14 − 7 = _____

	Across	Up
7.	9 − 1 = _____	11 − 5 = _____
8.	15 − 6 = _____	15 − 11 = _____
9.	12 − 2 = _____	11 − 9 = _____
10.	13 − 1 = _____	13 − 12 = _____
11.	15 − 5 = _____	10 − 9 = _____
12.	15 − 6 = _____	14 − 12 = _____

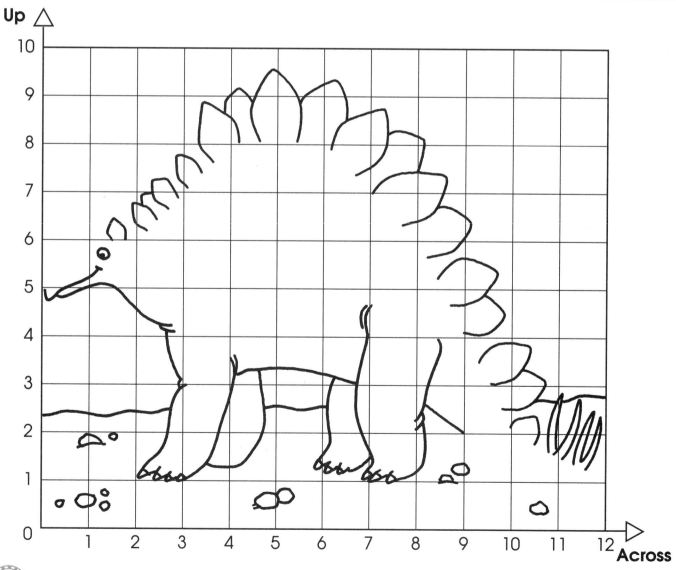

Up

Across

Name _____

Tropical Tree

1. Solve the problems.

2. Find each number pair on the graph. Make a dot for each.

3. Connect the dots in the order that you make them.

4. What picture did you make?

_____

	Across	Up
1.	10 – 5 = _____	7 – 0 = _____
2.	19 –12 = _____	9 – 4 = _____
3.	10 – 4 = _____	18 –11 = _____
4.	20 –12 = _____	8 – 2 = _____
5.	9 – 3 = _____	17 – 9 = _____
6.	18 –10 = _____	15 – 8 = _____

	Across	Up
7.	17 –11 = _____	19 –10 = _____
8.	20 –16 = _____	11 – 2 = _____
9.	19 –18 = _____	13 – 5 = _____
10.	20 –17 = _____	15 – 7 = _____
11.	20 –19 = _____	14 – 8 = _____
12.	18 –15 = _____	20 –13 = _____
13.	13 –12 = _____	16 –11 = _____
14.	17 –13 = _____	16 – 9 = _____

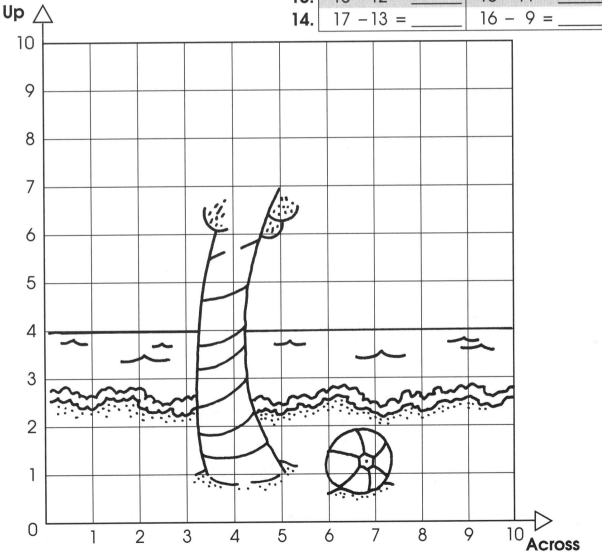

Name _____

Nine Lives

1. Solve the problems.

2. Find each number pair on the graph. Make a dot for each.

3. Connect the dots in the order that you make them.

4. What picture did you make?

_____

	Across	Up
1.	20 − 16 = _____	10 − 10 = _____
2.	13 − 7 = _____	20 − 20 = _____
3.	15 − 7 = _____	13 − 12 = _____
4.	17 − 8 = _____	17 − 14 = _____
5.	20 − 11 = _____	7 − 2 = _____

	Across	Up
6.	14 − 6 = _____	14 − 7 = _____
7.	20 − 12 = _____	18 − 9 = _____
8.	14 − 8 = _____	9 − 2 = _____
9.	19 − 15 = _____	19 − 12 = _____
10.	8 − 6 = _____	9 − 0 = _____
11.	17 − 15 = _____	12 − 5 = _____
12.	14 − 13 = _____	14 − 9 = _____
13.	6 − 5 = _____	7 − 4 = _____
14.	20 − 18 = _____	18 − 17 = _____
15.	11 − 7 = _____	0 − 0 = _____

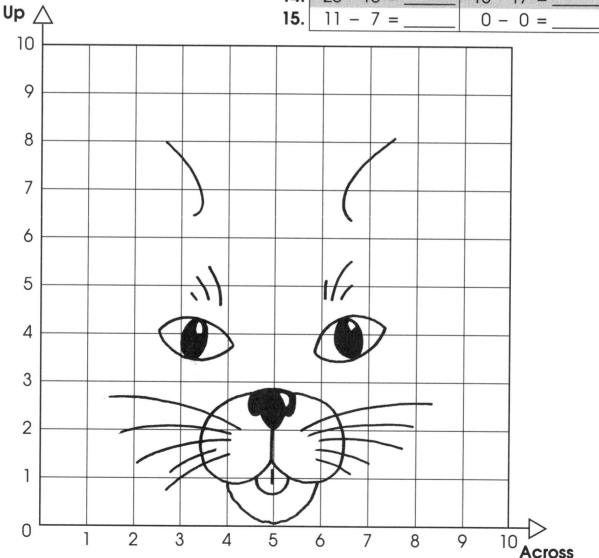

Name _____

Bubble Yum!

1. Solve the problems.

2. Find each number pair on the graph. Make a dot for each.

3. Connect the dots in the order that you make them.

4. What picture did you make?

_____

	Across	Up
1.	27 – 23 = _____	58 – 53 = _____
2.	18 – 15 = _____	23 – 21 = _____
3.	30 – 27 = _____	29 – 28 = _____
4.	18 – 11 = _____	46 – 45 = _____
5.	58 – 51 = _____	17 – 15 = _____
6.	28 – 22 = _____	49 – 44 = _____
7.	19 – 15 = _____	77 – 72 = _____

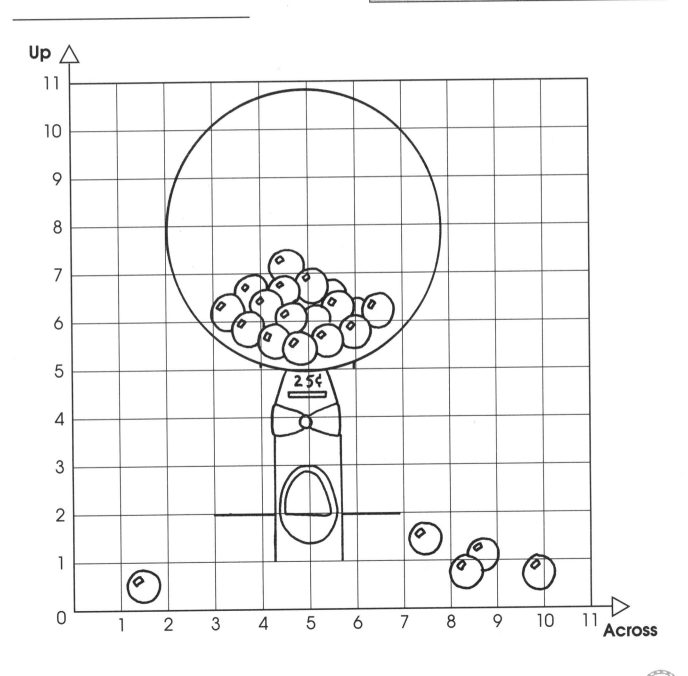

Name _____

Ding, Dong!

1. Solve the problems.
2. Find each number pair on the graph. Make a dot for each.
3. Connect the dots in the order that you make them.
4. What picture did you make?

_____

	Across	Up
1.	75 – 30 = _____	26 – 16 = _____
2.	57 – 17 = _____	93 – 73 = _____
3.	45 – 10 = _____	70 – 30 = _____
4.	88 – 58 = _____	56 – 11 = _____
5.	48 – 18 = _____	70 – 20 = _____
6.	39 – 14 = _____	79 – 29 = _____
7.	37 – 12 = _____	95 – 50 = _____
8.	26 – 6 = _____	79 – 39 = _____
9.	58 – 43 = _____	47 – 27 = _____
10.	65 – 55 = _____	61 – 51 = _____

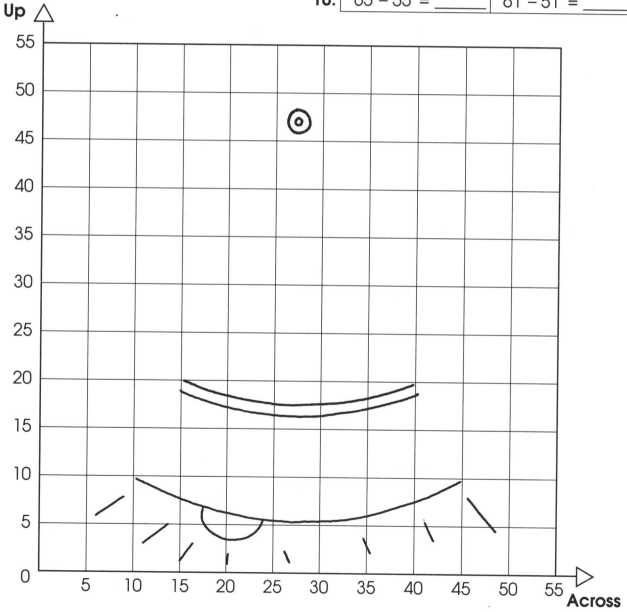

Great Graph Art to Build Early Math Skills Scholastic Professional Books

Name _____

Milk Delivery

1. Solve the problems.

2. Find each number pair on the graph. Make a dot for each.

3. Connect the dots in the order that you make them.

4. What picture did you make?

_____

	Across	Up
1.	46 – 38 = _____	27 – 19 = _____
2.	21 – 17 = _____	46 – 38 = _____
3.	42 – 38 = _____	50 – 18 = _____
4.	89 – 69 = _____	61 – 29 = _____
5.	70 – 50 = _____	47 – 19 = _____
6.	67 – 39 = _____	43 – 15 = _____
7.	61 – 29 = _____	33 – 13 = _____
8.	68 – 28 = _____	67 – 47 = _____
9.	51 – 11 = _____	47 – 39 = _____
10.	73 – 37 = _____	82 – 74 = _____

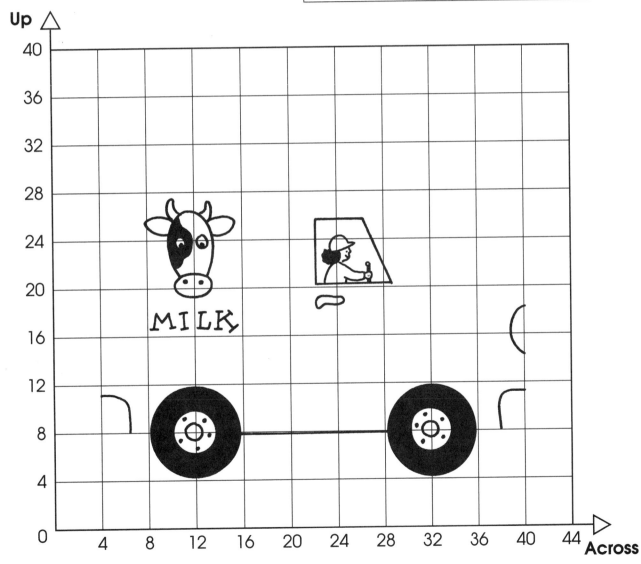

Make a Graph Art Picture!

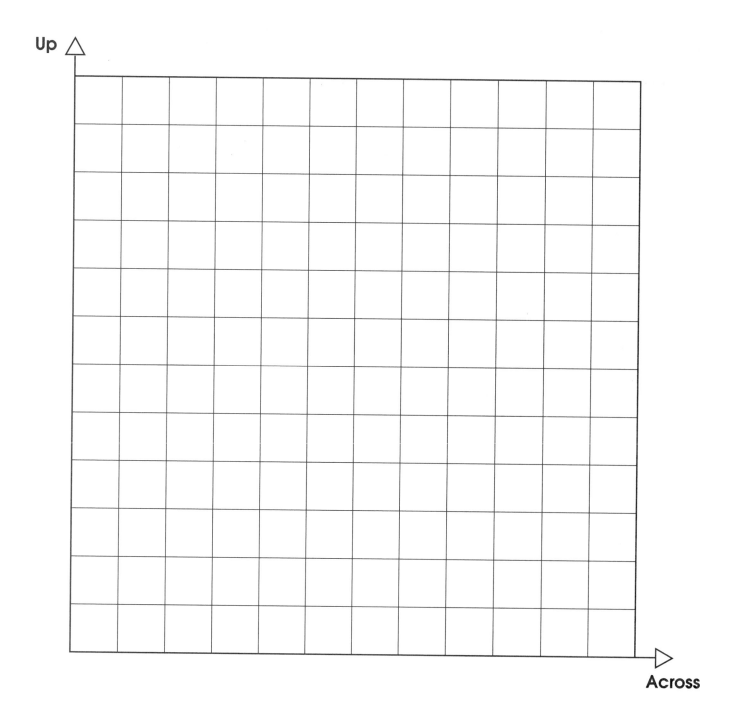

Up

Across

Great Graph Art to Build Early Math Skills Scholastic Professional Books

Answers

Page 7: **First Number**
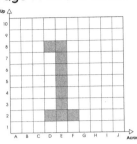

Page 8: **School Supplies**
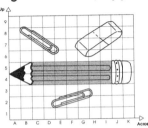

Page 9: **Giant Shovel**
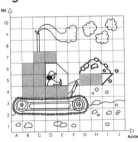

Page 10: **Make a Wish!**
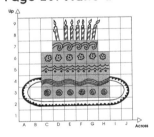

Page 11: **Wiggle Worm**
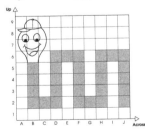

Page 12: **Friendly Greeting**
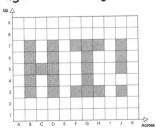

Page 13: **Man's Best Friend**
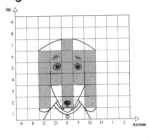

Page 14: **Mystery Letter**
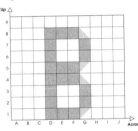

Page 15: **Your Move**
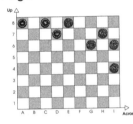

Page 16: **Off to School!**
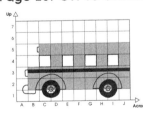

Page 17: **Skyline**
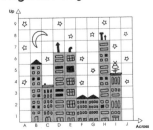

Page 18: **Home Sweet Home**
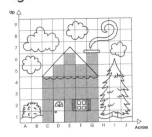

Page 19: **Just for You**
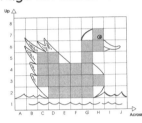

Page 20: **Beautiful Swimmer**
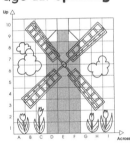

Page 21: **Spinning Around**

Page 22: **There She Blows!**
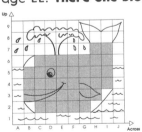

Page 23: **Sail Away**
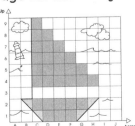

Answers

Page 24: **Spring Flower**

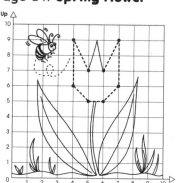

Page 25: **Bright Light**

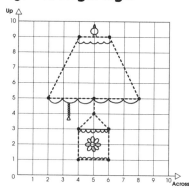

Page 26: **Tow Truck**

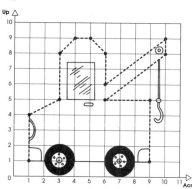

Page 27: **Love**

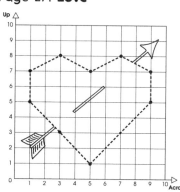

Page 28: **Yummy Treat**

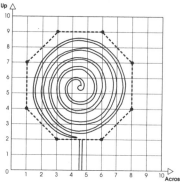

Page 29: **Just Hatched**

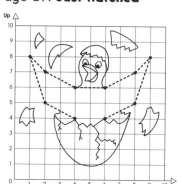

Page 30: **Surprises!**

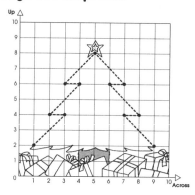

Page 31: **Let It Snow!**

Page 32: **Sparkling Diamond**

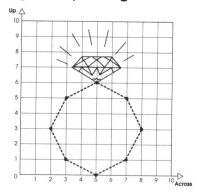

Page 33: **Out for a Swim**

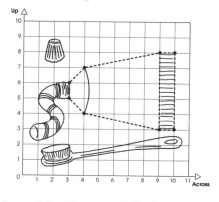

Page 34: **Bright Smile**

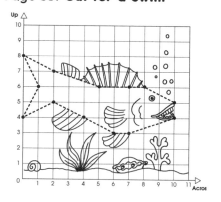

Page 35: **Stars and Stripes**

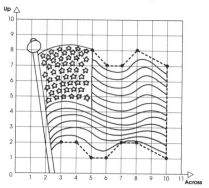

Answers

Page 36: **Sprinkles on Top!**

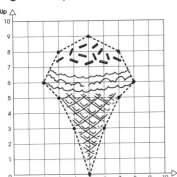

Page 37: **Chug, Chug**

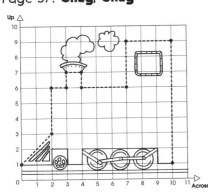

Page 38: **Night-Light**

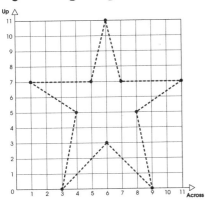

Page 39: **Rain Showers**

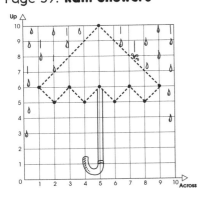

Page 40: **Funny Face**

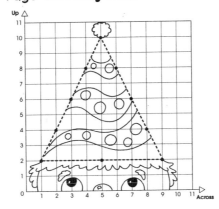

Page 41: **Teatime**

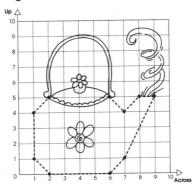

Page 42: **Curvy Letter**

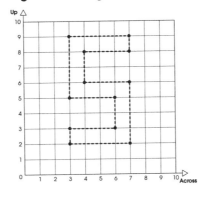

Page 43: **Measure Up**

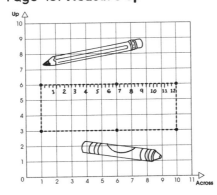

Page 44: **Highflier**

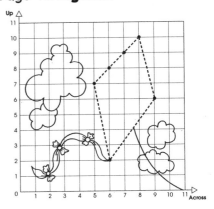

Page 45: **Juicy Fruit**

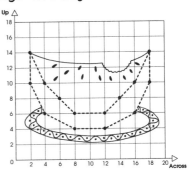

Page 46: **Slowpoke Reptile**

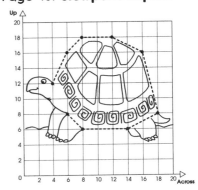

Page 47: **Horsing Around**

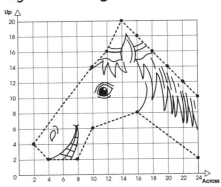

Answers

Page 48: **You've Got Mail!**

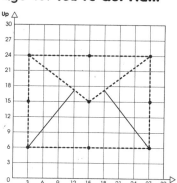

Page 49: **Home From the Beach**

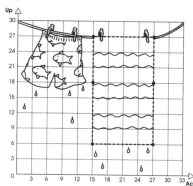

Page 50: **Zoo Animal**

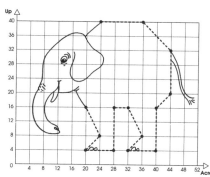

Page 51: **Rich Man's Fish**

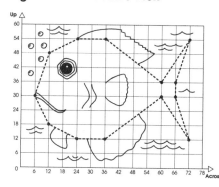

Page 52: **Let's Go for a Ride**

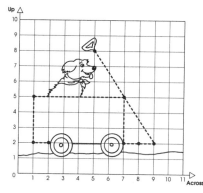

Page 53: **Chirp, Chirp!**

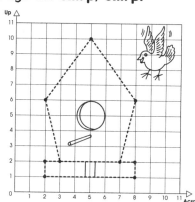

Page 54: **Out of the Past**

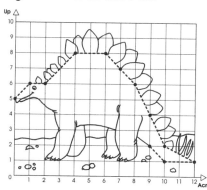

Page 55: **Tropical Tree**

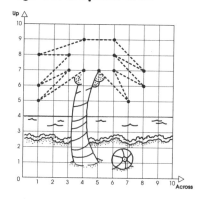

Page 56: **Nine Lives**

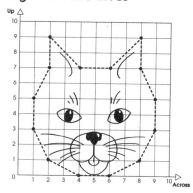

Page 57: **Bubble Yum!**

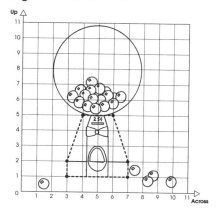

Page 58: **Ding, Dong!**

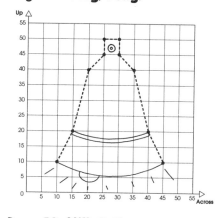

Page 59: **Milk Delivery**

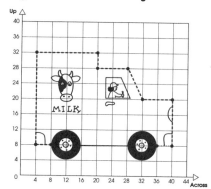